Wrenda Taylor

2π

From Pentecost to Patmos

FROM PENTECOST TO PATMOS

HIGHT C MOORE

Convention Press

NASHVILLE, TENNESSEE

Copyright, 1934 • The Sunday School Board

Southern Baptist Convention, Nashville, Tenn.

Reprinted, 1959 • CONVENTION PRESS

511-00206

This book is No. 0206 in Category 2, Section A.

Library of Congress Catalog Card Number: 59-9311

Printed in the United States of America
20. o 59 R.R.D.

About the Author

HIGHT C MOORE was born January 28, 1871, in Globe, North Carolina. He received the A.B. degree in 1890 from Wake Forest College, North Carolina, and attended Rochester Theological Seminary, New York (1893). In 1915 Wake Forest College conferred on him the D.D. degree, and in 1920 he received the Litt.D. from Baylor University.

Dr. Moore was ordained as a Baptist minister in 1890 and served churches in Morehead City, Winston-Salem, Monroe, Chapel Hill, and New Bern, North Carolina. In 1904 he became state Sunday school secretary of North Carolina; in 1907 he was employed as field secretary of The Sunday School Board of the Southern Baptist Convention. For ten Years (1907–17) he served as editor of the *Biblical Recorder*, Raleigh, North Carolina. In 1917 Dr. Moore became editorial secretary of the Baptist Sunday School Board, Nashville, Tennessee, where he served until 1943.

Dr. Moore was secretary of the Southern Baptist Convention for over thirty years (1914–46) and a member of the Executive Committee of the Southern Baptist Convention for seventeen years. He has also served as director of the American Theological Seminary, Nashville, Tennessee, as secretary-treasurer and editorial secretary of the International Council of Religious Education (1924–43), and as a member of the International Sunday School Lesson Committee.

For a number of years (1918–52) Dr. Moore wrote *Points for Emphasis*, an annual pocket commentary on the Sunday school lessons. He also wrote numerous books: *Seaside Sermons* (1892), *Select Poetry of North Carolina* (1894), *The Books of the Bible* (1902), *The Country Sunday School* (1905), *North Carolina Baptist Handbook* (1911, 1912), *The Man of Mark in the Church Tomorrow* (1912), *Style Book for Writers and Printers* (1918), *The Interwoven New Testament* (1931), *From Bethlehem to Olivet* (1934), FROM PENTECOST TO PATMOS (1934), *New Testament Biographies* (1935), *The Better Christmas* (1948), *Nuggets from Ridgecrest* (1950), and *Golden Texts* (1953). He wrote widely in denominational periodicals and pamphlets.

On May 2, 1893, Hight C Moore married Laura Miller Peterson. After his retirement in 1943, the Moores made their home in Ridgecrest, North Carolina, where he was active in the work of the Ridgecrest Baptist Church until his death in May, 1957.

Contents

Church Study Course for Teaching and Training

THE CHURCH STUDY COURSE for Teaching and Training began October 1, 1959. It is a merger of three courses previously promoted by the Sunday School Board—the Sunday School Training Course, the Graded Training Union Study Course, and the Church Music Training Course.

The course is fully graded. The system of awards provides a series of five diplomas of twenty books each for Adults or Young People, one diploma of ten books for Young People, two diplomas of five books each for Intermediates, and two diplomas of five books each for Juniors. Book awards earned previously in the Sunday School Training Course, the Graded Training Union Study Course, and the Church Music Training Course may be transferred to the new course.

The course is comprehensive, with books grouped into nineteen categories. The purpose of the course is to (1) help Christians to grow in knowledge and conviction; (2) help them grow toward maturity in Christian character and competence for service; (3) encourage them to participate worthily as workers in their churches; and (4) develop leaders for all phases of church life and work.

The Church Study Course for Teaching and Training is promoted by the Baptist Sunday School Board, 127 Ninth Avenue, North, Nashville, Tennessee, through its Sunday School, Training Union, Church Music, and Church Administration departments, and by these same departments in the states affiliated with the Southern Baptist Convention. A complete description of the course and the system of awards may be found in the *Church Study Course for Teaching and Training* catalog, which may be obtained without charge from any one of these departments.

A record of all awards earned should be maintained in each church. A person should be designated by the church to keep the files. Forms for such records may be ordered from any Baptist Book Store.

Requirements for Credit in Class
or Home Study

IF CREDIT is desired for the study of this book in a class or by home study, the following requirements must be met:

I. IN CLASSWORK

1. The class must meet a minimum of seven and one-half clock hours. The required time does not include assembly periods. Ten class periods of forty-five minutes each are recommended. (If laboratory or clinical work is desired in specialized or technical courses, this requirement may be met by six clock hours of classwork and three clock hours of supervised laboratory or clinical work.)

2. A class member who attends all class sessions and completes the reading of the book within a week following the last class session will not be required to do any written work.

3. A class member who is absent from one or more sessions must answer the questions on all chapters he misses. In such a case, he must turn in his paper within a week, and he must certify that he has read the book.

4. The teacher should request an award for himself. A person who teaches a book in section B, C, or D of any category or conducts an approved unit of instruction for Nursery, Beginner, or Primary children will be granted an award in category 11, Special Studies, which will count as an elective on his own diploma. He should specify in his request the name of the book taught, or the unit conducted for Nursery, Beginner, or Primary children.

5. The teacher should complete the "Request for Book Award— Class Study" (Form 150) and forward it within two weeks after the completion of the class to the Church Study Course Awards Office, 127 Ninth Avenue, North, Nashville 3, Tennessee.

II. IN HOME STUDY

1. A person who does not attend any class session may receive credit by answering all questions for written work as indicated in the book. When a person turns in his paper on home study, he must certify that he has read the book.

2. Students may find profit in studying the text together, but

individual papers are required. Carbon copies or duplicates in any form cannot be accepted.

3. Home study work papers may be graded by the pastor or a person designated by him, or they may be sent to the Church Study Course Awards Office for grading. The form entitled "Request for Book Award—Home Study" (Form 151) must be used in requesting awards. It should be mailed to Church Study Course Awards Office, 127 Ninth Avenue, North, Nashville 3, Tennessee.

III. CREDIT FOR THIS BOOK

This book is No. 0206 in category 2, section A.

Suggested Audio-Visual Materials

FOR USE IN TEACHING THIS BOOK

THE FOLLOWING LIST of audio-visual materials will be helpful in teaching this book. In some instances more material is listed than it will be practical to use. In such cases select the frames of the filmstrips and portions of motion pictures that contribute most directly to the chapters of the book you are teaching and that most nearly meet the needs of the group you are teaching.

Chapter 1

FILMSTRIP: *Paul, a Chosen Vessel*

Chapter 2

SLIDES: Ha 803 *Jesus Calls Saul on Damascus Road;* Ha 805 *Ananias Restores Saul's Sight*
FILMSTRIPS: *A Lost Pharisee; Chosen Vessels*
MOTION PICTURE: *Light from Heaven*

Chapter 3

SLIDES: Ha 811 *Barnabas and Saul Bring Relief for Poor of Jerusalem;* Ha 813 *Paul and Barnabas Sail to Asia Minor;* Ha 814 *Paul and the Pro-Consul Sergius Paulus*
FILMSTRIP: *Chosen Vessels*
MOTION PICTURE: *God's Care of His Own*

Chapter 4

SLIDE: N 241 *The Council at Jerusalem*
MOTION PICTURE: *Salvation and Christian Fellowship*

Chapter 5

SLIDES: Ha 817 *Timothy and His Mother;* Ha 820 *Paul Receives Macedonian Call;* Ha 821 *Lydia Learns of Jesus at the Riverside at Philippi;* Ha 822 *Paul and Silas Convert the Jailer at Philippi*
FILMSTRIP: *A Lost Jailer*
MOTION PICTURE: *What Must I Do to Be Saved*

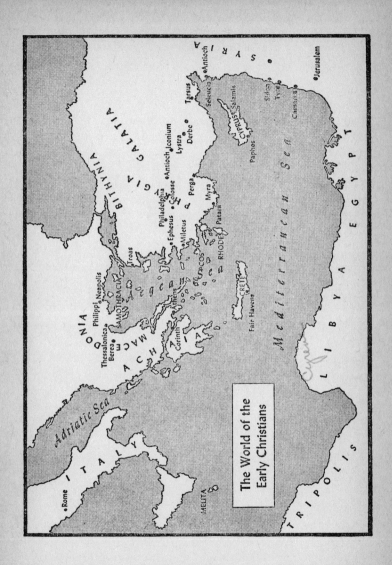

The World of the Early Christians

Brief of the Book of Acts

THE STORY of events from Pentecost to Patmos is the story of the spread of Christianity according to the pattern outlined by Jesus: "But ye shall receive power, when the Holy Spirit is come upon you: and ye shall be my witnesses both in Jerusalem, and in all Judaea and Samaria, and unto the uttermost part of the earth." [1]

The account centers around the life and works of Paul, the apostle to the Gentiles. Most of our information is given us by the historian, Luke, in the book of Acts. Some further details are gained from statements or inferences in the Epistles and the Revelation.

I. THE CHURCH AT JERUSALEM

TEXT: Acts 1:1 to 7:60
TIME: A.D. 30–35

For ten days the apostles and their fellow disciples waited in Jerusalem as the Lord had told them. Then the Holy Spirit came, Peter preached, and the three thousand converts were won. The church at Jerusalem, shepherded by the apostles and richly successful in its blessed work, was nevertheless the target of repeated persecution. Its internal work was also alternate shade and sunshine, the first shown by the judgment upon Ananias and Sapphira, and the second, by the appointment of the seven deacons and the consequent prosperity of the church. The rapidity of growth in the Jerusalem church is mentioned many times in the book of Acts (see for example 2:47; 4:4; 5:14; 6:1).

[1] Unless otherwise stated, the Scripture quotations in this book are from the American Standard Version, copyright by the International Council of Religious Education, and are used by permission.

1

II. THE MISSIONS ROUND ABOUT

TEXT: Acts 8 : 1 to 11 : 18
TIME: A.D. 35–41

The persecution at Jerusalem which culminated in the martyrdom of Stephen scattered the church membership into the region round about. Philip, the evangelist, penetrated Samaria and the South. Saul the Sanhedrist became Paul the preacher, the opening leaves of his record recounting his conversion, his experiences in Arabia, Damascus, and Jerusalem, and his settlement in Cilicia. Peter visited the neighboring cities of Lydda, Joppa, and Caesarea, performing miracles and preaching the Word.

III. THE CHURCH AT ANTIOCH

TEXT: Acts 11 : 19 to 12 : 25
TIME: A.D. 41–46

The church at Antioch in Syria, already founded and flourishing, grew rapidly under the joint ministry of Barnabas and Paul and their co-workers. To relieve the Judean brotherhood during foretold famine, a collection was taken at Antioch and forwarded by Barnabas and Paul, who brought back from Jerusalem the news of the martyrdom of James, the imprisonment of Peter, and the death of Herod Agrippa I.

IV. THE MISSIONS IN ASIA MINOR

TEXT: Acts 13 : 1 to 16 : 8
TIME: A.D. 47–50

From the great missionary church of Antioch in Syria went forth Barnabas and Paul with John Mark on the first tour to the island of Cyprus and to several cities in Asia Minor. After returning to Antioch, they went up to Jerusalem and attended a council there which settled the policy that Gentiles could become Christians without first becoming Jews. The second missionary journey of Paul extended from Syrian

Antioch as a base, westward through Asia Minor to Troas, the extremity of the continent.

V. THE FIRST CHURCHES IN EUROPE

TEXT: Acts 16:9 to 18:23
TIME: A.D. 51–53

The churches in Europe sprang up in the path of the apostle as, in obedience to the Macedonian vision, Paul proceeded in spite of persecutions to Philippi, Thessalonica, Beroea, Athens, and Corinth.

VI. THE CHURCH AT EPHESUS

TEXT: Acts 18:24 to 21:16
TIME: A.D. 53–58

The church at Ephesus holds the center of interest in Paul's third missionary journey. First came the eloquent ministry of Apollos. Then Paul appeared and labored for three fruitful years, his ministry closing in the uproar made by the shrine-makers of the goddess Diana. However, he carried out the plan already made to visit Greece, spending three months at Corinth. Returning, he met the Ephesian elders at Miletus and then continued his last journey to Jerusalem.

VII. THE MISSION TO ROME

TEXT: Acts 21:17 to 28:31
TIME: A.D. 58–66

Paul's mission to Rome was accomplished by a circuitous route. His arrest at Jerusalem was followed by a detention of two years at Caesarea. The voyage to Rome was featured by the wreck at the island of Malta. The first imprisonment of the apostle at Rome lasted more than two years. After release, he probably revisited his former fields and may have gone westward to Spain, as he had hoped. But soon the Neronian persecution of Christians arose, and the great apostle was speedily apprehended, imprisoned, and executed.

CHAPTER 1

I. A Native of Tarsus

1. His Name
2. His Ancestry
3. His Birth
4. His Birthplace
5. His Own Family
6. His Personal Appearance
7. His Citizenship
8. His Contacts

II. A Student at Jerusalem

1. From a University Center
2. To a Theological Seminary
3. A Sacred City
4. A Great Teacher
5. A Strict Curriculum
6. A Zealous Student
7. A Favorable Environment

III. A Citizen of the Roman Empire

1. The Meaning of Citizenship
2. How Citizenship Was Secured
3. The Privilege of Citizenship
4. Paul's Use of His Citizenship

IV. A Pharisee of the Strictest Type

1. The Heritage of a Pharisee
2. The Training of a Pharisee
3. The Life of a Pharisee
4. The Hope of a Pharisee
5. The Persecution of a Pharisee

1

SAUL

IN TARSUS

Acts 21:39; 22:3, 27–28; 26:4–7;
Philippians 3:3–6

Since tradition is not trustworthy and history is silent, it is to Paul himself that we are mainly indebted for authentic glimpses of his early life. Extracts from two of his speeches and from one of his letters give us most of what we know about him during this time.

I. A Native of Tarsus

1. *His Name*

It has been pointed out that every Roman citizen had three names—one each for the individual, the clan, and the family—as Marcus Tullius Cicero and Caius Julius Caesar. The citizen's proper name was the only one used, except for official purposes. We do not know two of the names that must have been given to the illustrious Tarsian at his birth.

Paul's name in Hebrew was Saul; and he was most probably named for the first king of Israel, who also was of the tribe of Benjamin. His Roman name, Paul, was a familiar one throughout the empire. For example, it was the deputy or proconsul at Paphos on the island of Cyprus whose name was Sergius Paulus. It is noteworthy that the apostle was known as Paul after his experience on Cyprus. The name was probably given him or taken by him by reason of his future contacts with the Roman world. The change was not indicative of a change of nature or career as with Abraham, Jacob, Daniel, and others. Since the apostle's cognomen was Saul in Hebrew and Paul in Roman, he was not spoken of under two names, as John Mark and Simon Peter.

2. His Ancestry

Paul's family belonged to the tribe of Benjamin, which furnished the first king for the Hebrew monarchy and always stood close to the royal tribe of Judah.

Again and again Paul says that he was a Jew. Concerning his father we have no personal history, but only a few legitimate inferences: He was a Pharisee, since Paul was the son of a Pharisee (Acts 23:6); he was a Roman citizen, so that Paul was freeborn (Acts 22:28); he appears to have had wealth enough to send his son to Jerusalem to school. It is thought that Paul's father was a native of Palestine and moved to Tarsus, where he was a merchant.

Concerning Paul's mother, absolutely nothing is definitely known. Undoubtedly, she was a true mother in Israel who transmitted her excellences to her son and carefully trained him in accordance with the highest Hebrew standards. Paul had a sister who lived in Jerusalem, and her son proved of great value to the apostle at a critical hour (Acts 23:16–22).

It is thought that Paul's ancestors settled in Cilicia about 175 B.C. Whether he was cast off by his family after his conversion is not certainly known, though he appears to have suffered "the loss of all things" for the sake of Christ.

3. His Birth

Paul was born probably four or five years after the birth of Jesus. He was a "young man" (probably about thirty) when Stephen was murdered. He was "Paul the aged" (sixty or more) when he wrote Philemon. It is not probable that he ever heard John the Baptist, or that he saw Jesus during his earthly ministry. It was earlier that Paul was a student in Jerusalem and later that he became the leading Sanhedrist in the city.

4. His Birthplace

Paul was a native of the Roman province of Cilicia, which was that portion of Asia Minor bordering on the northeast coast of the Mediterranean. It was a very fertile district. The wide plain was well watered. Vegetation was rank. The climate was hot in the summer. Snow-capped mountains rose on the western horizon. Indeed, the province was difficult of access by land. The Cilician Gates on the north are described as a narrow, crevasse-like cleft in the Taurus range, eighty-three miles long. There were two other approaches which were less difficult but highly protective against invaders. This region was conquered by Assyria in 854 B.C. It became a Roman province in 100 B.C., was reorganized by Pompey in 66 B.C., and made an imperial province in 22 B.C.

The city of Tarsus, where Paul was born, was an important city, though not of the first rank. It was the capital of the province and the metropolis in the midst of a fertile plain. It is said to have been built or fortified by Sennacherib, who located it on both banks of the river Cydnus, as Babylon stood on both banks of the Euphrates. Tarsus was only a few miles from the sea and the Cydnus was navigable to the cataracts just above the city. Since the city was thus open to the sea and was on the great trade route over land east and west, it was an emporium for trade. Many Greeks and Jewish merchants flocked to the city and thrived there.

Though populous and wealthy in the time of Xenophon, Tarsus probably reached its zenith of prosperity at the time of Paul's birth. It was a free city under Rome, which means that it was granted self-government and immunity from taxation. At one time it was the residence of Antony, who while here was visited by Cleopatra, who arrived impersonating Aphrodite.

Tarsus was also a renowned seat of learning. It was the original habitat of Stoic culture and ranked with the other two great university centers of the time at Athens and Alexandria. The languages freely spoken on its streets, in its shops and homes, were Greek, Syriac (or Aramaic), and Latin. Hebrew and other languages were, of course, taught and spoken in its schools. Since the days of Alexander, who three centuries earlier fought the decisive battle of Issus in its vicinity, Tarsus had been the meeting ground for East and West, and its population was partly Greek and partly Oriental. It was the best spot in all the earth to cradle the apostle to the Gentiles.

5. *His Own Family*

If Paul had a wife or children or a home of his own, there is no mention of it in the Bible. Some think that he never married. The prevailing view, however, is that he did marry, since it was a general requirement that young rabbis should marry about the age of twenty. He was a member of the Sanhedrin, if the "voice" he gave against Stephen was a formal vote; and, if so, he had been married (unless his betrothed had died). And yet if Paul was married, his wife seems not to have been with him during his apostolic career. It is possible that she left him when he gave up all for Christ, but many think that Paul was a childless widower and that as such he gave his counsel to the widows and unmarried at Corinth (1 Cor. 7:8).

6. *His Personal Appearance*

From his own words it may be inferred that Paul was not physically prepossessing and that his speech was not oratorically magnetic. If his "thorn in the flesh" was a bodily ailment—whether a disorder of the eyes or chronic malaria, or some form of epilepsy—it must have had its effect not only upon his bearing before an audience but also in his personal habits and comfort. Undoubtedly, however, Paul had the power of great physical endurance and achievement, for he suffered untold privations and trying experiences on sea and land, suffering scourging and hard imprisonment time and again. Not without a sinewy physique could one stand so great a strain for many years.

7. *His Citizenship*

Paul was not only a native and for years a resident of Tarsus, but he also held civic privileges there. This fact, of course, would imply that the family was well established in the city. As a boy Paul was taught a trade, and since goat's-hair cloth was abundant in the district, he was taught the use of it as a means of support. He was therefore adept in making tents, for which there was a wide demand, and no doubt he was able also to use the cloth in other forms, as sails, awnings, and the like. If his father was a merchant, as seems likely, Paul's own work would have been in line with the business of the family, which may have been part of a Jewish colony settled in Tarsus by Antiochus Epiphanes in 171 B.C.

Whether or not Paul attended the great university in Tarsus we do not know. It is thought, however, that his father, being a loyal Pharisee, may not have been quite liberal enough to patronize a pagan institution of learning. Still the influence of the student life of the city must have been great on the mind of Paul during his boyhood. At any rate, it was here that the decision was made that he should be a rabbi and take his regular theological course, although retaining his citizenship in Tarsus. His Roman citizenship was to play a significant part in later events of Paul's life.

8. *His Contacts*

Not during his whole career did Paul get away from the liberalizing influence of his native city. He was, of course, at home in dealing with the Hebrew multitude, as at Jerusalem. He was not the slightest ill at ease when he encountered the Roman captain, as he did on the castle stairs of the Tower Antonia. He seems to have known personally the Asiarchs at Ephesus. To his own Tarsian group belonged apparently the persons who were referred to by Paul as his kinsmen (Rom. 16:7, 21). So he could truly claim to be "a citizen of no mean city."

II. A STUDENT AT JERUSALEM

1. *From a University Center*

As we have seen, the city of Tarsus was one of the great university cities of the Roman world. If Paul did not register as a student there, he certainly received a profound and lasting impress from the Stoic philosophy, the Greek culture, and the Roman educational influences that radiated through its streets and environs. He was born and bred in a seat and center of culture.

2. *To a Theological Seminary*

The decision having been made that Paul should become a rabbi, he must be given better advantages than those of the local synagogue and different culture from that in the university of Tarsus. He was probably not more than thirteen years of age when he became a matriculate of one of the best, probably the very best, of the theological schools of his time. As Jesus went to Jerusalem at twelve years of age to become a "son of the law" and remained overtime with the great teachers in the Temple, so Paul at about the same age became also a "son of the law."

3. A Sacred City

The atmosphere of Tarsus was distinctly liberal, while that in Jerusalem was quite as definitely exclusive and narrow. Yet the Holy City stirred the heart of Paul as he entered its walls to prepare himself for his lifework. His mind must have been flooded with memories of the past of which he had read and heard in his home and synagogue. He thought of the prophets and kings who had lived and wrought and passed away. He wandered over the sacred sites and looked at the sacred buildings, some of them now only in ruins and some of them rising in magnificence. To him no city on earth was so sacred or so worthy as Jerusalem to be the place of his preparation for a useful career.

4. A Great Teacher

The fame of Gamaliel of Jerusalem had gone out everywhere. He was recognized as one of the greatest teachers of his time and since has taken his place as one of the greatest teachers of all time. Indeed, he has for centuries been regarded by the Jews as the first of the seven great *rabbans* (pre-eminent rabbis). Gamaliel was a grandson of the illustrious Hillel. He did not put any ban upon secular literature and learning. He was the recognized leader of the liberal school of Pharisees.

It was "at the feet of Gamaliel" that Paul received his rabbinic education. It was customary for the teacher to occupy a low platform while his pupils were seated in a circle on the ground at his feet. The schools and the universities in Egypt and other parts of the East have a similar arrangement to this day.

5. A Strict Curriculum

The studies in Gamaliel's great school were confined strictly to "the law of our fathers." The Scriptures of the Old

Testament were carefully studied and taught in their entirety and without any admixture of secular learning. The comments of the masters on the Old Testament were, of course, diligently studied. Indeed, the traditions of the elders were much sought after and highly prized. In addition, both students and teachers devoted much time to question and comment upon the sacred passages under consideration. There was a great deal of repetition involving "line upon line" and "precept upon precept." Of course, there was much rigid memory work, so that no one could complete his course without memorizing and mastering much of the Old Testament.

Through such a course Paul was carried in a strict manner, not only in accordance with the custom of the forefathers, but also according to the highest educational standards of his time.

6. A Zealous Student

As Paul entered his teens, he entered Gamaliel's great school. His mind was virgin soil for the good seed of the great teacher. He had lost no time upon other things. He had experienced no mental or moral waste by lapses in his life. With soul unsoiled and intellect keen and spirit yearning upward, Paul proved himself a pupil who was "zealous for God."

7. A Favorable Environment

Not only was there a great teacher on the platform and a great student in the group at his feet, but also there was a favorable atmosphere in the city and its environs. Paul knew his people. When, in later years, he spoke to them at Jerusalem as they were massed in a howling mob seeking his destruction, he thought back through the years to his own schooldays, and how he also had been a zealot. In both cases zeal was misdirected, but it set on fire the central and fundamental convictions of all who were "zealous for God."

III. A Citizen of the Roman Empire

1. *The Meaning of Citizenship*

As Rome conquered the world it annexed many nations to the empire. Generally it exacted tribute in money and slaves, but denied the electorate to subjugated peoples. Citizenship was at first enjoyed only by the patricians in and around the imperial city. In 337 B.C. citizenship was extended to plebeians as well. After a time citizenship was extended to residents of other countries. When one became a Roman citizen, the distinction was indicated by his name and the white toga.

2. *How Citizenship Was Secured*

One became a Roman citizen first of all by birth, as in the case of Paul. But *civitas* (citizenship) was often secured by purchase, sometimes at great cost. Sometimes it was secured by a great military feat, as soldiers today receive the Distinguished Service Cross. Now and then some act of loyalty was rewarded with citizenship. The distinction was awarded at first by the assembly at Rome and later by the autocratic favor of the emperor. The award was first made with great care and discrimination, but in later times the standards were lowered and the privilege widened to include numbers who did nothing to deserve it.

3. *The Privilege of Citizenship*

Every Roman citizen had the right of suffrage. He could hold property. He could aspire to public office. He had freedom from direct taxation. He was ordinarily exempt from physical punishment, and certainly so when uncondemned. He had the right of appeal to the emperor.

If one at any time should make a false claim to Roman citizenship, he would be subject to additional indignity, degradation, and punishment. If his claim were found true, he would be given the opportunity to substantiate it and also to receive its benefits.

4. Paul's Use of His Citizenship

As a citizen of the Roman Empire, Paul on a number of occasions claimed the privileges which were his due. It was so at Jerusalem when Captain Lysias saved him from the mob. It was so at Philippi when the politarchs realized the terrible blunder they had made in having him scourged. The governor of Achaia recognized the apostle's Roman citizenship during the disturbance at Corinth. The Asiarchs were fully aware of it during the uproar at Ephesus. Governors Felix and Festus made public mention of it at Caesarea, regarding the apostle's appeal to Caesar. The centurion Julius on the voyage to Rome guarded and regarded his illustrious prisoner as a Roman citizen.

And beyond his personal appeal to protection as a Roman citizen, Paul must have been profoundly influenced in his thinking because of his citizenship in the world empire of Rome. It had something to do with widening his horizon. It must have made its contribution to his imperialism of spirit and purpose. It helped make him cosmopolitan, for as a citizen of Rome he was a citizen of the world.

IV. A PHARISEE OF THE STRICTEST TYPE

1. The Heritage of a Pharisee

The Pharisee has come to stand for the sheerest formality and externalism in religion. But the origin of this famous sect was highly creditable to those who embraced it. It was during and after the exile that the Jews, then bankrupt in national power and spirit, were exposed to pagan influences. There was great necessity for separateness on the part of those who were true to the faith of their fathers. Hence, a band of devout Jews, small at first but later flourishing, virtually organized a rebellion against the secularization of Israel. They believed in the sacred mission of the Jewish race. They pleaded and wrought for a return to spiritual religion. They espoused a great cause and devoted themselves to it at whatever sacrifice. And even before the Maccabean period they exerted a powerful influence for the moral and spiritual uplift as well as the racial integrity and nationalization of the Jews. Into such an heritage Saul of Tarsus was born.

2. *The Training of a Pharisee*

As the son of a Pharisee who kept the faith in a foreign city and as a descendant of a line of Pharisees of whom any youth might be proud, Paul was carefully trained and instructed after the strict manner of his fathers. Not only was pure pharisaic blood in his veins, but also he was trained with diligence at his mother's knee and by his home hearth and in his father's place of business, as well as in the synagogue of Tarsus.

When the time came for Paul to receive his higher education in a distant city, he was sent straight to the best school of the Pharisees to be found on the planet. It was in charge of their greatest rabbi, and there through a rigid course the gifted young Tarsian received the best theological training of his time, and doubtless the best training in the Mosaic law available at any time in the history of the world.

3. *The Life of a Pharisee*

We cannot think of Saul of Tarsus as being simply a student and a scholar. He tells us plainly that he lived the life of a Pharisee. No one could have surpassed him in fidelity to the minutest details of the ritual he had learned from Gamaliel. Like the Pharisee of the Temple, Paul must have fasted often and given tithes of all he possessed. In his personal and professional life, in his private and public affairs, he exemplified the strictest adherence to his faith and reached the highest standard of his sect. He was probably the finest exponent of the righteousness of the scribes and Pharisees.

4. The Hope of a Pharisee

As long as he lived, though he rejected the externalism of the Pharisee, Paul never forsook the hope of a Pharisee, which involved belief in the resurrection from the dead. His belief was in striking contrast to that of the Sadducees, who did not believe in a future life and practically were atheists. In striking contrast, Paul declared, "I am a Pharisee!" According to one writer, "Had he withdrawn his membership from the religious society of the Pharisees, his action would have been a blow at the scriptural doctrine of the resurrection of the dead." He never relinquished that hope. Indeed, he found its true basis and fulfilment in the resurrection of Jesus from the dead.

5. The Persecution of a Pharisee

It was not the higher puritanism of the Pharisees that Jesus criticized or that Paul ultimately renounced, but their externalism and hypocrisy. The better elements of the sect were finally overwhelmed by baser elements, which like an eating cancer devoured all that was good in their teachings. Thus the Pharisee became a partisan, and he could not endure the alleged rivalry of Christianity. So Saul, probably after years of synagogue service in Tarsus, and upon his return to Jerusalem, possibly as a member of the Sanhedrin, began a vigorous persecution of the churches in the hope of utterly stamping out Christianity from the earth. His dedication to his goal cannot be questioned. After his conversion he looked back with a sense of deep pain upon his activities as a persecutor of the church.

When Paul became a convert to Christianity and a missionary of many years' standing, he was called upon to taste the bitter cup which he had pressed to the lips of others.

FOR CLASS ACTIVITIES AND FURTHER STUDY

Question-Answer Study [1]

Where was Saul born? Of what race were his parents? Of what sect of that race? What citizenship did he inherit? Point out Tarsus on the map. What river flowed through it? How far was Tarsus from the sea? Why were the cities of the Old World built on rivers and at some distance from the sea? What was the importance of Tarsus commercially? Politically? Intellectually? What was its relation to the Roman Empire? How long did Saul live in Tarsus? How did the city influence his life? At what age did Saul's elementary education begin? What subjects did he study? For what profession did his parents prepare him? Why must he learn a trade? What trade did he learn? At what age did he go away from home to school? Where did he go? Who was the teacher? As Paul reached maturity, therefore, what equipment did he have? What has this to do with his subsequent usefulness?

Suggested Topics for Assignment-Report Conference [1]

Saul's Parentage
Significance of Tarsus in Paul's Life
Scholars of Tarsus
Saul's Preparatory Work
Saul and His Trade
Saul and Gamaliel
The Sect of the Pharisees
Roman Citizenship—Acquisition and Importance
Saul's Equipment for Service

Research Activities

The author makes allusions to the following persons from secular history. Using a good encyclopedia, seek to learn who each was and some significant facts about each in relation to Paul's background: Pompey; Sennacherib; Xenophon; Alexander, the Great; Antiochus Epiphanes; Gamaliel.

[1] The "Question-Answer Study" and the "Suggested Topics for Assignment-Report Conference" were prepared by Dr. John L. Hill.

CHAPTER 2

I. PERSECUTION
1. Concern About Religion
2. Controversy for Judaism
3. Conflict with Christianity
4. Conscience Concerning Christ

II. PENITENCE
1. Conviction Felt
2. Contrition Shown
3. Confession Made
4. Command Received
5. Compliance Given

III. PRAYER
1. Ananias at Prayer: Service
2. Saul at Prayer: Salvation

IV. PROFESSION
1. Enlightenment
2. Enlistment
3. Equipment

V. SAUL'S EARLY MINISTRY
1. Beginnings in Damascus
2. Retirement in Arabia
3. Return to Damascus
4. Visit to Jerusalem
5. Settlement in Cilicia

2

SAUL
IN DAMASCUS

Acts 9:1–31

THE CONVERSION OF SAUL was epochal in the history of the early churches. It occurred about A.D. 36 on the highway approaching Damascus from the south. Armed with requisite authority from the high priest in Jerusalem, and with a bloody record already set, Saul was on his way to the metropolis of Syria, determined to stamp out Christianity from the oldest city in the world. But just as he caught sight of his prey and was panting with rage, the persecutor met the Persecuted in light outdazzling a Syrian noonday, and came to terms in his complete surrender to Jesus the Christ as Saviour and Lord. Thereupon, Saul arose from the ground a new man and groped his way into Damascus, there to be enlightened by the evangelist whom he had intended to destroy and to begin the ministry that was to evangelize the Roman Empire and at last be crowned with martyrdom.

I. PERSECUTION

1. *Concern About Religion*

Saul of Tarsus had not lived an immoral life from which it was necessary that he be converted in order to be outwardly a good man. As a matter of fact, he was "righteous" in every accepted sense of the term at the time. He was a believer in God, an interpreter of the Bible, a leader in his race which boasted of being the Chosen People, and ardently he held the doctrines and the hopes of his people. He was devoted to the Jewish code. He not only believed in the rules and regulations of his faith, but held himself in strict conformity to them even in minutest detail. He was thus deeply concerned about religion and desired that the whole world be won to the Pharisaism so dear to his own heart.

2. Controversy for Judaism

While the young Sanhedrist believed in God and the Bible as embodied in the Old Testament, he did not believe in Jesus as the Messiah. Though praying daily for the coming of the Christ and hoping ardently for the deliverance of the Jews from conquerors who had enslaved them for five centuries, Saul took his stand firmly against the teaching that the Messiah had already come in the person of Jesus of Nazareth. Indeed, he felt it his duty, as he said to Agrippa, actively to oppose the name of Jesus the Nazarene.

Upon his return from Tarsus to Jerusalem, Saul attended the service in the Cilician synagogue where the Greek-speaking Jews from his own province congregated and worshiped. It was in this synagogue that Stephen, one of the seven deacons, was accustomed to speak. Most likely Saul heard Stephen address the crowd, declaring that the Messiah had come, that he was none other than Jesus of Nazareth, and that his crucifixion had been accomplished by the Romans at the instigation of the Jews. The meeting being open, there is hardly doubt that Saul did immediately and vigorously protest against such doctrine. In the debate that followed, the subtleties of Stephen's opponents, probably including Saul, were no match for the ardent deacon's spirit. Everybody present recognized Stephen as the victor.

At once Stephen's opponents determined to do more than debate with such an enthusiast. They must stamp out every vestige of his doctrine. Stephen therefore was arraigned before the Sanhedrin and condemned for blasphemy. But he made before that august court his memorable defense, which Saul undoubtedly heard. The persecutor certainly saw Stephen stoned to death, his face radiant as that of an angel, and his last words being a prayer for his enemies as he called fervently on the Lord Jesus.

3. *Conflict with Christianity*

The persecution that arose soon after Pentecost did not deter Christians from activity everywhere they went. Indeed, Saul on his return to Jerusalem after an absence of several years in Tarsus—during which period Christ had been crucified and Pentecost had come—was amazed at the magnitude of the Christian movement. To learn that three thousand persons had been converted to Christianity in a single day and to learn further that the Christian community in Jerusalem had grown to five thousand, was something amazing to the young Sanhedrist. Moreover, he had found that the Christian religion was actually being called "the Way," which was understood to be the way of the Lord, the way of salvation, the way of the better life, a new and living way, fulfilling the Master's own words, "I am the way" (John 14:6).

The animosity of Saul was unbounded. He leveled his lightnings against what he regarded as unpatriotic and dangerous doctrine. Without delay he became a chief inquisitor and terror king. Like a very dragon breathing out fire and death he exhaled menace and murder. He literally made havoc of the church, the word "havoc" suggesting "wild boars uprooting tender vines." He went into all the synagogues in search of "heretics." He actually invaded the privacy of every suspected home. He dragged both men and women in chains before the bar of alleged justice. He arraigned them in the synagogues and caused them that believed to be beaten (scourging being a recognized synagogue punishment). He thrust them into prison. He sought to make them blaspheme the name of Christ. He voted for the death sentence of some and saw that they were actually put to death. In short, he was "exceedingly mad" against Christians, and with excessive ardor he sought to destroy every one of them and every vestige of their faith.

So it was that the zealous persecutor sought authority from the high priest—who was probably Jonathan, the son of Annas, since Caiaphas, the son-in-law of Annas, had been deposed in A.D. 35. Under that authority Saul was permitted by Roman law the power of seizure and punishment in synagogues where the Sanhedrin had jurisdiction. Other cities than Jerusalem therefore could be searched for believers in Christ. After Pilate's removal, the Sanhedrin either assumed or was given the right to put one to death. It is certain that Aretas, king of Arabia, which at that time included Damascus, was favorable to the Jews. Saul therefore had no difficulty in securing the proper papers authorizing him to pursue his bloody task in Damascus.

There was a large influential Jewish population in Damascus, and it is said there were at least thirty synagogues flourishing there at the time. The city was a veritable paradise almost surrounded by desert. From the Anti-Lebanon mountains descended the crystal waters of the Abana (now called Barada) River, flowing directly through the metropolis and running itself dry in the desert beyond.

Damascus was a great commercial center on the highway between the great valleys in central Asia and the Nile Valley in northern Africa. It had about it the flavor of antiquity. It was a great city in the days of Abraham. It was one of the prized possessions of Solomon. For centuries it was the chief city of Syria. It came under the sway of Alexander the Great.

It was the capital of a province under Roman rule. Saul was convinced that such a city must be rid of the Christian doctrine. Apparently this could be done with ease, since Christians seem at the time to have retained their membership in the synagogues, where they could be readily detected.

The associates of Saul on the journey to Damascus constituted perhaps only a small retinue of possibly fifteen to twenty-five men. He would need their protection and aid in handling prospective prisoners. The journey of one hundred thirty-six or one hundred forty miles would take about six days by caravan. Though the artists picture the company as riding horses, it is more likely that only donkeys were used on the expedition. Possibly Saul himself rode a donkey, but many think that he made the journey afoot, since he was led by the hand as he entered the city. It has been suggested that the luggage of the party was carried on donkeys.

4. Conscience Concerning Christ

While Saul was so bitter and bigoted in his attitude toward Christianity, there can hardly be any doubt that within his own heart there was uncertainty and doubt concerning his course. He had been brought up in a liberal atmosphere at Tarsus. He had come under the tolerant influence of Gamaliel at Jerusalem. Could he ever forget the face and the words of Stephen at his martyrdom? What if the Christians were right? After all, could it be that Jesus was the Christ as Stephen averred? At all events, the character of Christians under fire must have impressed Saul profoundly. The arguments he had heard respecting the Messiah did not seem defective in the light of the Old Testament. Did the imperfections of the law as observed with pharisaic devotion furnish a background for the Christian faith? Perhaps on his long journey northward Saul heard the voice of conscience concerning Christ. At any rate, during his great crisis he was told, "It is hurting you to keep on kicking against the goad" (Acts 26:14 Williams).[1] Surely resistance was vain!

II. PENITENCE

1. Conviction Felt

As Paul and his party were approaching Damascus, possibly in the immediate vicinity or perhaps at the traditional spot ten miles southward where they came within their first view of the city, there was a downflashing of light that dazzled and stunned. It was about noon, when travelers ordinarily take their siesta, but the persecutor was pressing forward. The light was above the brightness of the sun. Yet it was not sunlight, nor was it a flash of lightning. It was evidently like the light that flamed on the mount of transfiguration, or like the burning bush that attracted Moses on the backside of the desert, or like the Shekinah glory that filled the Temple of Solomon.

In that light Saul actually saw Jesus as the risen and glorified Christ. Later he wrote, "Have I not seen Jesus our Lord?" (1 Cor. 9:1). It was as actual as any other appearance of the risen Lord—as, for example, the appearance that convinced Thomas the doubter. It was not like Paul's vision of the man of Macedonia. Both Ananias and Barnabas stated that Saul had actually seen the Lord. It was thus that he learned that he had not been opposing an imposter but the Son of God. Under no sunstroke was the persecutor humbled, but by a miracle which involved his whole afterlife and his relation to Christ. The story of his conversion was one of Paul's strongest arguments for Christianity.

---

[1] All Scripture quotations from Williams, throughout this book, are from *The New Testament in the Language of the People* by Charles B. Williams (Chicago: Moody Press, 1955) and are used by permission of the publishers.

2. *Contrition Shown*

The heavenly effulgence was attended with an urgent call, twice repeating his name. "Saul, Saul!" The same voice had in the olden times said, "Abraham, Abraham!" and also "Samuel, Samuel!" The same voice in the person of the Nazarene had called "Martha, Martha!" and also "Simon, Simon!" Moreover, the voice arraigned the foe of the Christian faith, "Why persecutest thou me?" Is it any wonder that Saul fell to the ground? So did Daniel and Ezekiel in the ancient day. So also did every member of Saul's party. But they fell stunned while he fell under a great conviction. His was a cry of deepest reverence, "Who art thou, Lord?" Could anyone be more contrite?

3. *Confession Made*

The prostrate Sanhedrist was immediately given the greatest of all divine revelations "I am Jesus whom thou persecutest." And the message was given not in Latin or Greek but in Hebrew (or Aramaic, the form then in use), the everyday language of the Jews. Let the persecutor know that the Persecuted was infinitely greater than he. "It is hard for thee to kick against the goad" (Acts 26:14). Moreover, the living Lord was identified with his followers. Any persecution of them was persecution of him, and any good to even the least of them was good done unto him.

Trembling and astonished at what he saw and heard, Saul came at once to the critical point in his career. He made a complete and unconditional surrender of himself to Christ: "Lord, what wilt thou have me to do?" (Acts 9:6 AV).

4. *Command Received*

There was not much for Saul to do at the moment, though his whole afterlife was involved, and indeed the whole future history of Christianity. The first thing was simply, "Arise"; for God does not despise the contrite, and he will lift up the fallen. The next thing, "Stand upon thy feet" (Acts 26:16); for one must become erect in his inner life and be in the attitude of progress. The third thing, "Enter into the city"; for the journey must be completed—though not as originally planned. Then came the promise, "And it shall be told thee what thou must do"; for God uses human means in carrying on his great purposes.

The attendants of Saul were, of course, utterly astounded. They saw the light but did not see Jesus. They heard the sound of the voice ("sound" and "voice" being the same word in Greek) but not the words which were uttered. Like their leader, they fell to the ground and were fixed on the spot where they stayed (the meaning of "stood") until aroused to continue the journey.

5. Compliance Given

While the surrender of Saul to the will of God occurred on the highway and was sudden, he did not reach the joy and peace of assurance and acceptance until three days later. His entrance into the city was quite different from what he had planned. When he opened his eyelids he found himself blind, and he remained sightless for a time. He had actually to be led by the hand into the city. Apparently he did not deliver his papers from the high priest. He went, possibly according to previous appointment, to the house of Judas on Straight Street. Here Saul went to his room and remained without food or drink for three full days. It was a time not only of abstinence but of meditation. He must have experienced a profound spiritual struggle. His whole life had collapsed in his collision with Christ. Now there must be reconstruction and rebuilding around a new center—which center was Jesus Christ.

III. PRAYER

As Peter and Cornelius were prepared each for the other on the Mediterranean coast, so now Saul and Ananias were prepared for each other in Damascus.

1. *Ananias at Prayer: Service*

Ananias of Jerusalem was a hypocrite, but not Ananias of Damascus. Luke the historian here calls him a disciple, and there is no finer distinction for anyone. He was probably the Christian leader in the city. Speaking of him later, the apostle referred to him as a pious man (Acts 22:12) who though humble was holy; a man who carefully and conscientiously obeyed the law; a Christian man who bore a good reputation among all the Jews of the city.

Evidently Ananias was in intimate fellowship with his Master, for he kept within speaking distance of the Lord all the time. Hence, the appearance of the Lord to him occurred as if it were in the natural order of things, although he did not have actual sight of Jesus as Paul had near Damascus, but simply a vision as Peter had on the housetop of Joppa. When the Lord spoke to Ananias, he responded without hesitation as Isaiah answered his call amid the glory of the ancient Temple.

The command which came showed how minutely the Lord is acquainted with each of his servants. Ananias may have been a citizen of no special distinction, and yet the Lord called him by name. And the Lord not only knew the city in which both the evangelist and inquirer resided, but he also named the street, the house, the name of the inquirer, his birthplace, and precisely what he was doing at the moment. Explicit directions were but a sand grain along the beaches of infinite knowledge.

Ananias probably did not live on Straight Street, which

was about two miles long, extending through the city from the east gate to the west gate, flanked in ancient times with Corinthian columns, and being a thoroughfare of world re- nown. The traditional house of Ananias is in another part of the city.

The hesitation of the good man was precisely what might be expected. He knew of the record of the persecutor in Jerusalem and other towns. He was aware, apparently, that Saul had come to Damascus armed with authority to make havoc among the Christians there. It may seem strange that the servant would show more concern than the Master for the safety of believers. Yet the hesitation was temporary.

The divine purpose concerning the persecutor was clearly revealed. The Lord had appointed Saul to know his will, and Saul was now doing it; to see the righteous One and hear him speak as he had done on the highway south of the city; to be a witness for Christ among all men, and particularly to be a chosen vessel bearing his name to the Gentile world; and finally to suffer for the cause of Christ as perhaps no one ever suffered except the divine Sufferer at Golgotha.

So the good Ananias in his communion with God learned anew the secret of service. And he found, as many other dedi- cated Christians have found, that the tiny light of a humble life may kindle the wick which causes another to shine as a lighthouse in the kingdom.

2. Saul at Prayer: Salvation

"Behold, he prayeth!" That was the word of the Lord to Ananias concerning Saul, and it showed that he was now a saved man, earnestly seeking light and leading from the Lord. It showed to Ananias further that there is no danger in a praying man, no matter how bigoted nor how bitter he was aforetime in his antagonism: "For [because], behold, he prayeth."

The record does not show the subject or sentiment embodied in Saul's prayer. There must have been deep remorse, for again and again during his lifetime he expressed regret for his anti-Christian efforts. Certainly he was deeply agitated over the experience that had come to him. His whole past with its theological training and ecclesiastical standing must be adjusted to new conditions. What must he do immediately in Damascus? What must he do when he went back to Jerusalem? How could he best invest his life in the days to come?

We have the answer that came to the persecutor who had been changed into a penitent and now a believer engaged in earnest prayer. Rather singularly we are indebted for it to Ananias, who received it from the Lord. During his blindness and abstinence, Saul in happy vision saw a man bearing the name of Ananias and coming to him, laying hands upon him so that he might receive his sight. Had Saul ever prayed effectually before that time? There is no record of it. But now the answer came as a fountain from which flowed a stream of blessing adown the years.

IV. PROFESSION

1. *Enlightenment*

Ananias had been enlightened, and so he was ready to be a light to another in distress. At the word of the Lord he departed from his home without delay and without fear. Direct to Straight Street he went and entered into the house of Judas. Perhaps he was acquainted with Judas. Most probably he had never seen the young Tarsian. But both the visitor and the visited knew that Ananias had received divine direction as to what now was to be done. With tender sympathy Ananias stretched forth his hands and laid them on the blinded Sanhedrist, who may have been lying prostrate upon his couch in a dark room.

The words of the good man were balm to a troubled heart.

The very first note was one of utmost fraternity: "Brother Saul." So Ananias gave a brother's welcome to one who had come north to make havoc of the church. The second word was one of the clearest identification. Ananias told Saul that he had been sent on this errand by "the Lord, even Jesus, who appeared unto thee in the way which thou camest."

Apparently, Saul had told no one of his experience. And certainly he had had no communication with Ananias. The identification of Jesus as the Lord who had appeared alike to the evangelist and the inquirer was complete. Then followed the promise of the two greatest blessings that the heart of Saul could desire: the first, that he might receive his sight; and the second, that he might be filled with the Holy Spirit. Thus and thus alone could his greatest physical and spiritual need be supplied.

Nor was the blessing long delayed in its bestowal. Indeed, it occurred straightway: "And all at once something like scales fell from his eyes" (Acts 9:18 Williams). That was the sensation Saul experienced, and Luke uses the medical term which was common in the literature of the day. The restoration of sight, however, was unlike the removal of a cataract but very definitely a miracle. So also was the infilling of Saul with the Holy Spirit. He had observed Pentecost as a Jewish feast, but now he knew its meaning and experienced its spiritual thrill and vitality.

2. Enlistment

Saul had been truly converted and also filled with the Holy Spirit. He was therefore a candidate for the ordinance of baptism. He knew of the custom of the churches. He was also informed of his duty by Ananias. The new Christian did not hesitate. Immediately he arose and was baptized. Most likely Ananias baptized him. The ordinance may have been performed in a pool in the court of the house of Judas or in the Abana River, which probably was only a few rods away.

At any rate, the apostle was buried with Christ in baptism in impressive symbol that his sins had been washed away.

3. *Equipment*

The great change had taken place in Saul's spiritual life. He was even now adjusting himself in his thinking on theological subjects. The physical nourishment which he took afforded him strength for the next step and was a type of his larger preparation for fellowship with the Damascus saints in their program of progress for Christianity.

Without delay the new convert began his ministry, to the joy of believers and the astonishment of the Jews, declaring that Jesus of Nazareth is the Son of God. The apostle proclaimed salvation by him who died and rose again and lives forevermore. He avowed devotion to the risen and reigning Christ as the living Lord. He professed allegiance to him in spreading the gospel to all nations. At length he would fulfil the prophecy of the Lord to Ananias: "I will show him how many things he must suffer for my name's sake."

V. SAUL'S EARLY MINISTRY

1. *Beginnings in Damascus*

Proclamation of Saul's new-found faith immediately followed his baptism. During his stay in Damascus he preached in the local synagogues, declaring that Jesus of Nazareth is the Son of God. The disciples were amazed at the marvelous change which had taken place in the archpersecutor of the churches. But steadily he grew in power, aiming his shafts particularly at the Jews, with proof incontrovertible that Jesus is the promised Messiah.

2. *Retirement in Arabia*

Preparation for further ministry was made during the period of retirement in Arabia. Saul may have gone not far east of Damascus or possibly to the Sinaitic peninsula with its rich historic associations. Here he may have remained most of the three years intervening between his departure from Jerusalem as a persecutor and his return as a preacher. The time was probably occupied with a restudy of the Scriptures as fulfilled in Jesus, an entire readjustment of his theological thinking, the discipline and development of a soul before the mercy seat, and perhaps the exercise of a special ministry among the Arabians.

3. *Return to Damascus*

Persecution followed Saul's return to Damascus. He preached so effectually that he raised the ire of the Jews, who would not accept his doctrine but could not answer his argument. They took up against him the weapon he had laid down. Deliberately, they planned to kill him, and they watched the city gates day and night in order to accomplish their purpose. Information, however, reached Saul in time for him to escape martyrdom through the aid of his fellow disciples, who by night let him down over the wall in a basket.

4. *Visit to Jerusalem*

Presentation to the disciples in Jerusalem occurred during Saul's fortnight in that city. At first the brethren were afraid of him because they doubted his discipleship. But when Barnabas introduced Saul, telling of his remarkable conversion and of his fearless ministry in Damascus, they gladly welcomed him into their fellowship. So effectually did he preach to the Greek-speaking Jews—the very company he was in when they strove with Stephen—that, in their inability to answer him, they actually plotted his death. At the request of the brethren and by divine direction, Saul left Jerusalem to fulfil a wider ministry among the nations.

5. Settlement in Cilicia

Proclamation of the gospel throughout Cilicia and in all that region followed Saul's settlement for four or five years in his native city of Tarsus.

FOR CLASS ACTIVITIES AND FURTHER STUDY

Question-Answer Study

What was Stephen's position in the early church? What was the charge against him? What was his defense? Describe his martyrdom. What was Saul's connection with Stephen's death? What was the effect of the persecution under Saul's leadership?

Where was Damascus? What do you know of its history? What was the purpose of Saul's errand to Damascus? By whom was he commissioned? Tell in your own words just what took place on the Damascus road. What preparation was made for Saul's reception in Damascus? What was Ananias' service to Saul? What was Saul's first act after his sight was restored?

What was the main emphasis of Saul's first preaching? Why did the Jews get angry? How did Saul escape from Damascus? Who vouched for Saul when he sought to join the disciples in Jerusalem? Does this incident throw any light on the manner of receiving members into the church?

Suggested Topics for Assignment-Report Conference

Saul and Stephen
The First Persecution
Saul's Noontime Experience
Effect of Saul's Conversion upon the Churches

Research Activities

Select a number of the outstanding conversion experiences recorded in the Bible, such as that of Matthew (Matt. 9:9), the Ethiopian eunuch (Acts 8:26–39), Lydia (Acts 16:13–15), the Philippian jailer (Acts 16:25–34). Compare each with the experience of Saul on the road to Damascus. What elements common to all these experiences are essential in every conversion?

CHAPTER 3

I. MINISTRY IN ANTIOCH

    1. Organization: Founding of the Church
    2. Instruction: Ministry of Barnabas and Saul
    3. Benevolence: Famine Fund for Judea
    4. Enlistment: Assistance of John Mark
    5. Missions: Call of Barnabas and Saul

II. MISSIONS IN SEVEN CITIES

    1. Salamis
    2. Paphos
    3. Perga
    4. Antioch (in Pisidia)
    5. Iconium
    6. Lystra
    7. Derbe

III. RETURN TO ANTIOCH IN SYRIA

    1. Revisitation on the Way
    2. Report upon Arrival

3

PAUL

IN ANTIOCH AND
ASIA MINOR

Acts 11:19–30; 12:25 to 14:28

THE PERSECUTION AT JERUSALEM that culminated in the stoning of Stephen scattered the disciples into many parts of Palestine and Syria. Many of them doubtless stopped in nearby cities, hoping to return to Jerusalem when the storm of hate subsided; but some of them traveled as far as Phoenicia, the rich province skirting the coast, and Cyprus, the great island in the eastern part of the Mediterranean Sea, and Antioch, the populous Syrian city situated on the river Orontes a few miles from its mouth.

I. MINISTRY IN ANTIOCH

1. *Organization: Founding of the Church*

The migration to Antioch was perfectly natural since, with a population of nearly half a million, it was at the time one of the greatest cities of the Roman world, only Rome and Alexandria standing ahead of it.

Founded by one of Alexander's generals in 301 B.C., Antioch was the center of commerce in a rich region and the capital of the province. In earlier days it had been the residence of the Seleucid kings; now it was the headquarters of the Roman governors of Syria and a favorite resort of the Roman emperors. The groves of Daphne near the city made it a famous seat of licentious idol worship. It was also an educational center, having a great library and a school of philosophy.

The chief distinction of Antioch lies in the fact that here the most vigorous of the early churches was founded and flourished, sending out streams of refreshment among the nations.

The first preachers arriving at Antioch from Jerusalem intended to confine their ministry to the Jews in the city. But others in the company who hailed originally from the island of Cyprus, some sixty miles westward, and from the city of Cyrene on the north coast of Africa, addressed themselves to work among the Grecians. Other Christians had, here and elsewhere, wrought among the Greek-speaking Jews, but now for the first time the Greeks were directly addressed.

It was a new phase of work, registering an advance upon anything hitherto attempted, and it was attended with divine blessing. "The hand of the Lord was with them: and a great number believed, and turned unto the Lord" (Acts 11: 21 AV).

Thus the church at Antioch was established with a mixed membership of Jews and Gentiles who wrought together harmoniously and effectively, winning many converts and exerting great influence.

2. *Instruction: Ministry of Barnabas and Saul*

Tidings of the wonderful work at Antioch reached the mother church at Jerusalem, whose members, while doubtless gratified at the founding of Christianity in a new center, were nevertheless filled with anxiety lest the new church should be rent by discordant elements, filled with all sorts of error, and corrupted if not overswept by the paganism around it. They therefore determined to send a fraternal messenger to Antioch with a view to offering all needed encouragement, counsel, and help.

Far the best man to go on this mission was Joseph, who by his fellow disciples had been named Barnabas because he was such an excellent exhorter. He was a Levite, and thus acceptable to the Jewish element in the churches both at Jerusalem and Antioch. He was a native of Cyprus, and doubtless had many acquaintances in the Syrian capital. He was familiar with the Greek language, and must have personally known a great many Greeks, and thus would be welcome to the Gentile element introduced into the membership at Antioch.

Barnabas had won distinction as a generous contributor to the benevolences of the church at Jerusalem. He had vouched for Paul, who on his return from Damascus to Jerusalem desired to join the disciples in their work. He had won reputation as "a good man, and full of the Holy Spirit and of faith."

When Barnabas reached Antioch, he was delighted with what he saw: an active, united, and growing church in the heart of a pagan city. His first word to its members could be nothing else than a message of encouragement. He "exhorted them all, that with purpose of heart they would cleave unto the Lord."

An evangelistic campaign followed, as a matter of course; and we may well assume that great crowds were attracted by the winsome personality, the fine hortatory powers, the profound piety, and the gospel messages of Barnabas. As a result, "much people was added unto the Lord."

To such proportions the work soon grew that Barnabas found himself unequal to the demands upon him. He must have help, and help of the right kind. In particular, a coworker was needed who was a teacher, an organizer, and a missionary.

Barnabas believed that the man for the place was Saul of Tarsus—born in the capital of the province of Cilicia; son of Greek-speaking Jews who were loyal to the ancient faith, his father being a strict Pharisee; a Roman citizen by inheritance; educated first at Tarsus, which was a university center, and then in theological lore at Jerusalem under the guidance of the great Gamaliel; honored almost certainly with membership in the Sanhedrin; disgraced by his highhanded persecution of Christians, but gloriously converted; ministering in the face of persecution both at Damascus and Jerusalem; and now in the prime of life as a preacher in his native region.

So the immediate task was to bring the fit man to the field of need. Unwilling to trust the mission to another who, not having the personal influence, might be unsuccessful. Barnabas himself made the trip from Antioch to Tarsus in order to enlist Paul in the work at Antioch and bring him at once to a work that could not wait. Soon Barnabas found the gifted Cilician, induced him to leave his native city, and together they came to Antioch to enter upon their joint ministry there.

With natures and gifts complementary and with the hearty co-operation of the church membership, Barnabas and Paul labored unremittingly and with great success in the Syrian capital. The campaign was under the auspices of the assembled church, laid special emphasis upon teaching, reached a great many people, and lasted a whole year (probably A.D. 44).

Public attention was so attracted by the activity and achievements of the church under its aggressive leadership that the disciples in their loyalty to Christ now first received the designation of "Christians"—a term evidently applied by outsiders, since no believers at that time would have been so bold as to assume a title embodying the name of the Lord. The Romans were probably responsible for the appellation by simply adding their "ian" to the Greek word "Christ," which in turn represented the Hebrew word for "the

Anointed One"; so that as the triple inscription on the cross introduced Christ to Romans, Greeks, and Hebrews, so the designation given to his followers included in its very nomenclature the people of power, of culture, and of morality.

3. Benevolence: Famine Fund for Judea

While things were going well with the growing church in the prosperous city of Antioch, the shadow of dearth and famine was discerned by the prophets of Jerusalem, some of whom came to Antioch and bore the ominous intelligence.

The most prominent of these prophets was Agabus who, under impulse of the Spirit, delivered the definite prophecy of the famine which actually took place right away (perhaps A.D. 45), and so during the reign of the Emperor Claudius (A.D. 41 to 54).

Unless relief was sent in good time, such a dearth was sure to work untold hardship and suffering in the church at Jerusalem, which was already heavily burdened with its charity work and doubtless liberally supported the apostles in their ministry.

In view of this situation, the church at Antioch determined to make a contribution for the relief of the brotherhood at Jerusalem. Every man in the membership was called on to give according to his ability, and the offering must have been creditable to the generosity of the givers. It is very likely that the contribution from Antioch included food as well as money.

The amount was sent to Jerusalem by Barnabas and Paul, brethren beloved by both the churches concerned, and their errand of relief was pleasing to the saints alike at Antioch and Jerusalem.

Some scholars maintain that Titus was in the group at this time (Gal. 2:4). If so, the present experience may have trained him for similar work in Achaia on behalf of the fund for the poor of Judea (2 Cor. 8:6).

4. *Enlistment: Assistance of John Mark*

How long the relief committee from Antioch remained in Jerusalem we are not told, but it was until after "they had fulfilled their ministration" of discriminating and affectionate distribution of the funds entrusted to them. This was done through the elders or the leading men of the church, the apostles evidently being absent from the city. That other things featured in the visit is likely, for the Jerusalem saints would have other use for hortatory Barnabas and logical Paul than to receive money at their hands.

There can be no doubt that Paul and Barnabas explained the situation at Antioch and told of the revival in that city and the outreach of Christianity to the Gentiles. Moreover, they must have given much consolation to the church at Jerusalem, so lately bereaved by the death of James, who had been killed with the sword, and by the imprisonment and subsequent flight of Peter from the metropolis.

At any rate, when the time came for the messengers to return to Antioch, John Mark, a kinsman of Barnabas, perhaps a native of Jerusalem and a prominent worker in the church there, accompanied Barnabas and Paul to Antioch, from whence he was to attend them on their missionary journey.

5. *Missions: Call of Barnabas and Saul*

The church at Antioch, as we have seen, was a center of evangelism, as is evident from constant ingathering; a school of Bible study, as shown in the whole year of instruction following Paul's arrival; and a seat of philanthropy, as seen in the relief funds sent to the famine sufferers in Jerusalem and vicinity. It was not, therefore, singular that in this great church there should have arisen a number of prophets, speaking authoritatively and perhaps foretelling events, and also teachers who carefully instructed the people in the ways of truth and righteousness.

The names of several of these prophets and teachers are preserved to us (Acts 13:1). Barnabas heads the list, and naturally, for he had won the place of leadership in the church by his faithful labors and great success. Of Symeon, whose surname was Black, we only know what is involved in his registration here. Lucius from the north African province of Cyrene was possibly a kinsman of Paul and one of the founders of the church at Antioch. Manaen had the distinction of having been brought up at court as the play-mate and foster brother of Herod Antipas, who disgraced his reign by murdering John the Baptist. The list closes with the name of Paul who, though probably the last to join the company, soon rose to first place in the missionary work of the church.

While these leaders, and doubtless their co-workers, were ministering unto the Lord in prayer and various other acts of devotion and in the spiritual exercise of physical fasting, they received a distinct revelation from the Holy Spirit. And the revelation was a singling out for special work of the two most brilliant and beloved men in the entire church: "Separate me Barnabas and Saul for the work whereunto I have called them." Barnabas and Saul—could the church spare them from its work? Yet the Spirit had now called them to be missionaries as truly and as distinctly as he had called them to their special ministry in Antioch. And the will of the Spirit must prevail.

So the church, acting affirmatively on the Spirit's sugges-tion, designated Barnabas and Paul for the foreign field and held an impressive ordination service which included fasting and prayer, the laying on of hands, and the benedictory fare-well. Never has there been a more significant setting apart of chosen workers for chosen fields.

Not only did Barnabas and Paul set out from Antioch with the blessing of the church, but also and especially were they "sent forth by the Holy Spirit," who after calling them to

the new task now directed their steps. So from Antioch they
went down the Orontes Valley sixteen miles to the seaport
city of Seleucia, whence they sailed to the island of Cyprus,
sixty or more miles westward.

II. Missions in Seven Cities

1. *Salamis*

Reaching the eastern shores of Cyprus, the native country
of Barnabas, the residence of perhaps a number of Paul's
acquaintances from nearby Cilicia, and the home of many
Jews and of some Christians who had been converted at
Pentecost, the two missionaries began work in the city of
Salamis.

As was wise at the moment and customary afterward, the
point of contact was through the Jews, who were so numerous
in the city as to have a number of synagogues. In these synagogues the word of God was preached by Barnabas and Paul,
and possibly also by John Mark, who was their attendant
on the tour.

How long the missionaries stayed and what success they
had are not recorded; but on leaving, they began a thorough
canvass of the country, not proceeding directly through the
island length of one hundred and fifty miles, but zigzagging
across it, visiting many important points, until they reached
Paphos, the seat of government on the western shore.

2. *Paphos*

Here was won the first convert under Paul's ministry whose
name is given. He was none other than the Roman proconsul,
Sergius Paulus, who was the governor of the province at that
time.

It appears that a hanger-on at court, and one who had
great power over the proconsul, was the professed magician
and pretended prophet known as Elymas, who was a Jew

bearing the name of Bar-Jesus. The governor, as a man
of intelligence, wished to hear from Barnabas and Paul the
word of God. But when he summoned the missionaries before him, Elymas opposed them in the distinct and spiteful
effort to prevent the governor from accepting their message.
However, Paul, being filled with the Holy Spirit, fastening
his eyes upon the sorcerer, called him in righteous anathema
a son of the devil and an enemy of all that is right and pro-
nounced upon Elymas a temporary blindness which would
lay bare his falsity and authenticate the missionaries.

As the pretender, with eyes darkened and hands stretched
out groping for a guide, turned away, the truth set forth by
Barnabas and Paul found its way to the heart of the proconsul, who believed in Christ and received with glad amaze-
ment the doctrines of the gospel. The climax and close of the
present Cyprian mission, this remarkable conversion must
have been heralded throughout the island and must have
exerted great influence toward the upbuilding of Christianity
there.

3. Perga

Sailing northward from Paphos, Paul and his comrades
proceeded across the sea and seven miles up the river Cestrus
to Perga, the principal city of the province of Pamphylia.

It was from this point that John Mark, for some reason
or other—a reason that was not acceptable to Paul—turned
back from the tour and returned to his home in Jerusalem.
It is possible that he was unwilling to face the perils of
Pamphylia, for its rivers were dangerous and its mountains
were infested by bandits, and missionary work would be attended with extreme difficulty.

At any rate, from Perga, where the stay seems to have been
brief and apparently without missionary effort until later,
Paul and Barnabas went on alone to their next station in
the tableland of central Asia Minor.

4. *Antioch (in Pisidia)*

The important highland city of Antioch had attained the rank of a Roman colony, and along with its native population contained many Romans, Greeks, and Jews. Soon after Paul and Barnabas arrived, they entered the local synagogue one sabbath, and when opportunity was given for remark Paul arose and delivered the first of his recorded sermons. It was new doctrine to the Pisidians, and request was made that it be further discussed the following sabbath.

When the next sabbath arrived and almost the whole city had assembled to hear the missionaries, the Jews in a fit of jealousy contradicted Paul in blasphemous language. Whereupon with all boldness he declared to them: "It was necessary that the word of God should first be spoken to you. Seeing ye thrust it from you, and judge yourselves unworthy of eternal life, lo, we turn to the Gentiles." This brave and decisive step was of course gratifying to the Gentile population of Antioch, who "glorified the word of God: and as many as were ordained to eternal life believed" (Acts 13:48). The incident naturally attracted widespread attention, and thus "the word of the Lord was spread abroad throughout all the region."

However, trouble was to arise from another quarter. Through the influence of the Jews who agitated the matter, certain women of high position and even the leading citizens of Antioch were so incensed at the missionaries that they expelled them from the city and province. As they left, Paul and Barnabas shook off the dust of their feet as a testimony against the persecuting Pisidians. Their next stop was in a neighboring province some forty-five miles away.

5. *Iconium*

At the foot of the Taurus Mountains nestled Iconium, an important commercial city of the province of Lycaonia. Here

Paul and Barnabas "entered together into the synagogue of the Jews, and so spake that a great multitude both of Jews and of Greeks believed."

But the work so auspiciously begun was not to continue. The unbelieving Jews roused the Gentiles by poisoning their minds against the missionaries. As a result, though Paul and Barnabas spent a long time at Iconium in a fearless ministry of both preaching and miracle-working, the people of the city as a whole were sharply divided in their allegiance between the Jews and the apostles. The opposition, including both Jews and Gentiles, not being above foul play, determined to maltreat and stone Paul and Barnabas.

But before the forming plot could be carried out, the intended victims were told of it and fled, perhaps about twenty miles, to another city in the same province.

6. *Lystra*

The capital of Lycaonia, located on the great Roman highway from Antioch in Pisidia, was Lystra, of which little is known beyond what is recorded in connection with Paul's missionary journeys. Since apparently there was no synagogue there, Paul and Barnabas preached either in some home or school or in the market place.

One of those who heard Paul was a man who had never walked, being lame from birth, and who sat in the streets of Lystra, certainly a familiar figure and possibly a well-known beggar. Seeing that he had the faith to be healed, Paul shouted to him, "Stand upright on thy feet." Instantly he leaped up and walked.

The people who witnessed the miracle said to one another in their local dialect that gods had come to them in the form of men. Barnabas, the more impressive physically, was styled Jupiter, and Paul was named Mercurius, since he was the chief speaker. The report thus started, without the knowledge of Paul and Barnabas, sped through the city and gained such credence and momentum that soon the local priest of Jupiter with a great following of people came with bullocks and garlands in order to offer sacrifice to the distinguished visitors. Horrified when they heard of it, Paul and Barnabas rent their clothes and ran in among the people and restrained them from the sacrifices they were about to make.

And now occurred one of those remarkable changes of opinion which show the fickleness of human nature. The men who had barely been able to keep the people from worshiping them speedily became the target of unreasoning hate. The Lystrians were stirred to animosity by certain Jews who followed the missionaries from Antioch and Iconium in order to cripple their influence if not actually to incite their assassination. The mob turned against the preachers, and "they stoned Paul, and dragged him out of the city, supposing that he was dead." When, however, the disciples gathered around his prostrate and bleeding body, he revived and rose up and returned with them to the city, whence he and Barnabas departed the next day.

7. Derbe

A few hours' travel along the Roman highway brought the missionaries to the city of Derbe, where without apparent interference and with great success they preached the gospel and taught many. It is likely that Gaius of Derbe, who was in the company attending Paul on his last visit to Jerusalem (Acts 20:4), was one of the converts at this time.

III. RETURN TO ANTIOCH IN SYRIA

1. Revisitation on the Way

From Derbe, Paul and Barnabas could have readily proceeded direct to Tarsus and thence to their starting point in Antioch of Syria. Instead, they turned back from Derbe and deliberately retraced their steps to a seaport beyond the mouth of the river Cestrus. They went, in turn, to Lystra where Paul had been stoned, to Iconium where an assault had been planned upon them, to Antioch from which they were expelled, and to Perga where now the way was open before them.

As they went, they confirmed the souls of the disciples with exhortations to perseverance, since only through tribulations are we to enter into the kingdom of God. In every church also they ordained the chosen elders with prayer and fasting, commending them to the Lord.

Thus the churches were established and organized for effective work.

2. Report upon Arrival

From the port of Attalia on the Gulf of Pamphylia, Paul and Barnabas, without revisiting the churches in Cyprus, sailed direct to Antioch in Syria "from whence they had been committed to the grace of God for the work which they fulfilled."

The church was immediately called together and the returned missionaries "rehearsed all things that God had done with them, and that he had opened a door of faith to the Gentiles." It was a marvelous story which must have thrilled and rejoiced the hearts of the congregation first hearing it from the lips of Paul and Barnabas.

For a considerable time—perhaps as much as two years—Antioch was now the residence of the missionaries who had made the first inroads upon the Gentile world.

FOR CLASS ACTIVITIES AND FURTHER STUDY

Question-Answer Study

Why did the Christians leave Jerusalem? How far north did they go? Locate Phoenicia, Cyprus, and Antioch. To what classes was the gospel preached? Was there anything particularly strange about this? Why was the church at Jerusalem disturbed by such tidings? Who was sent to investigate? What kind of man was he? What was his spirit? After seeing for himself, what exhortation did he give to the people? Why was Saul summoned to Antioch? How did he and Barnabas spend the year? Why were the disciples called Christians? How did the disciples anticipate the needs of their brethren in Jerusalem? Who were sent as fraternal messengers? Why did Herod kill James and imprison Peter? Describe Peter's deliverance from prison. Who accompanied Barnabas and Saul back to Antioch?

What local considerations would naturally make the Antioch church sympathetic toward missions? Who were the leaders in the church? What was the church doing when the Holy Spirit issued his orders? Whom did he select for missionary service? How did these men compare in ability with the other members? What formal sending off did the church give them?

Trace the entire course of the first missionary journey. What uniform practice did the missionaries follow in each community and with practically what result? Who is mentioned as Paul's first convert? In what capacity did John Mark accompany them? Where did he turn back? How did Paul meet opposition in Paphos? Outline the sermon that Paul preached in Pisidian Antioch. What was the occasion of Paul's proclaiming his mission to the Gentiles? What caused the embarrassment of Paul and Barnabas at Lystra? How did they meet it? Who camped on the trail of Paul and Barnabas for the greater part of this first journey? What was their motive? What follow-up work did the missionaries do before returning to the home church? Describe the welcoming service.

Suggested Topics for Assignment-Report Conference

Flight of Christians from Jerusalem
Northern Points Reached
Investigation by Barnabas
Barnabas and Saul in Antioch
Relief for Jerusalem Brethren
Herod's Persecutions
The Return to Antioch
Antioch in Christian History
Character of Barnabas
Antioch the Missionary Center

The Commissioning of Missionaries
The First Missionaries
Original Missionary Methods
Persecutions and Embarrassments of the Missionaries
Successes and Joys of the Missionaries
The Geography and History of Paul's First Missionary Journey
Paul's First Recorded Sermon
The Motive for Foreign Missions
Our Responsibility in the Light of Present Conditions

Research Activities

Read Acts 11:22–26. Find from verse 26 the ministry which Saul (Paul) and Barnabas emphasized during their year's work at Antioch. Trace some results of this intensive teaching ministry:

1. The distinctive character developed in those who were taught (They were so different they acquired a nickname.)
2. Good race relations fostered (Acts 11:27–30)
3. Church leadership developed (Acts 13:1)
4. A missionary spirit built up (Acts 13:2–3)

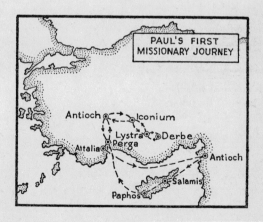

PAUL'S FIRST MISSIONARY JOURNEY

CHAPTER 4

I. THE QUESTION

    1. Raised by Judaizers
    2. Taught Salvation by Works
    3. Opposed by Paul and Barnabas
    4. Referred to the Apostles and Elders
    5. Messengers on the Way
    6. Reception in Jerusalem
    7. Opposition by Christian Pharisees

II. THE COUNCIL

    1. The High Personnel
    2. The Tense Discussion
    3. The Argument of Peter
    4. The Report of Barnabas and Paul
    5. The Judgment of James

III. THE DECISION

    1. The Vote of the Church
    2. The Messengers from Jerusalem
    3. The Letter to Gentile Churches
    4. The Presentation at Antioch

IV. LEADERS IN THE NEW DAY

    1. Judas and Silas
    2. Paul and Barnabas

4

PAUL

IN JERUSALEM

Acts 15:1–35

CARRYING OUT the Great Commission on their first tour through Cyprus and Asia Minor, Paul and Barnabas began making disciples of all nations. Their labors resulted in the conversion of many Gentiles as well as Jews who, upon their profession of faith in Christ, were baptized and admitted to the fellowship of the churches.

When the missionaries returned to their base in Antioch in Syria, they were confronted with certain teachers who, claiming apostolic approval, criticized the admission of Gentiles into the churches simply on the basis of their faith in Christ, and even went so far as to aver that circumcision was essential to salvation.

As a matter of fact, Paul and Barnabas, having been led by the Holy Spirit, were themselves competent to decide upon the matter, as they had already done. Certainly the church at Antioch could exercise its own authority in the settlement of this question. Yet it was thought best to refer the problem to the apostles and elders at Jerusalem for their consideration and counsel.

Accordingly, the council at Jerusalem heard the messengers from Antioch, deliberated at some length, and rendered a decision that has been memorable in the annals of Christianity. It broke the fetters of legalism in religion. It eliminated the doctrine of salvation by works and declared the doctrine of salvation by grace through faith. It magnified Christ as the Saviour of all who believe in him, whether Jew or Gentile, Greek or barbarian, bond or free. At the same time it recognized the leadership of the Holy Spirit, the independence and interdependence of the local churches, and the inspiration and authority of the Word of God in all matters of faith and practice.

So the report of the council at Jerusalem as brought back by messengers and letter to Antioch emphasized a cardinal tenet of Christian faith and inaugurated a new era in Christian missions.

I. The Question

1. *Raised by Judaizers*

A Judaizer has been defined (Robertson) as "a Jewish Christian who felt the Gentiles could not be saved without becoming also Jews." In his view the convert must retain his old Jewish faith and simply add to it the new faith that Jesus is the Messiah. The Judaizers thought, therefore, that to be a Christian one must be a Jew in faith and practice.

Undoubtedly news of the work of Paul and Barnabas in Asia Minor as to admitting Gentiles into the Christian churches had reached the mother churches in Jerusalem and Antioch. Very likely from the highlands of central Asia Minor many Jews had come to the Passover in the spring of A.D. 48. They would certainly not hesitate to let people in Jerusalem know what was occurring in their home country.

So it was that "certain men came down from Judaea" to Antioch in Syria. Paul later declared that they were "false brethren" (Gal. 2:4) for they were false in their claim of apostolic authority and false in their doctrine and false to the best interest of the churches to which they belonged.

Yet they "taught the brethren"; that is, they began teaching and kept it up for quite a while. They may have been contentious, as certainly they afterwards became, but at all events they were earnest and persistent, though apparently not very successful in the liberal atmosphere of the Syrian metropolis.

2. Taught Salvation by Works

The Judaizers professed themselves glad that Gentiles were becoming Christians, but they insisted that the only way to enter the Christian fold was through Judaism. They felt that that was the only way to prevent paganism from suffocating Christianity. It is possible that these Judaizers regarded as exceptional the conversion of Cornelius the Roman centurion and his baptism by Peter in accordance with special revelation. But they would be puzzled over the admittance wholesale of Gentiles into the churches on no other condition than their profession of faith in Christ.

Was not circumcision commanded of God? Was it not in its institution linked with the great name of Abraham? Was it not a fundamental in the ceremonial laws given through Moses? Did not their Bible once and again command it? Even so, it was never an essential to salvation. Though Jesus himself was subject to circumcision, he did not include it in his Great Commission and never mentioned it as necessary to the new birth or the new life. Moreover, the ceremonial law was not of universal and perpetual obligation. Nor was circumcision to be regarded as an act of merit.

Hence the gross error in the slogan of the Judaizers in Antioch: "Except ye be circumcised after the custom of Moses, ye cannot be saved." Here was a definite attempt to substitute the law of works for justification by faith. It held that messianic salvation could be procured through Mosaic ritual. But such a thing was just as impossible then as baptismal regeneration or salvation is impossible now. The basal demand then and today was for inward, moral cleansing, and not outward, ceremonial purifying—a circumcision of the heart and not of the flesh.

If the false teachers at Antioch had had their way, Christianity would have been simply a sect of Judaism and not a free, forward-looking, world-conquering force for Christ.

3. *Opposed by Paul and Barnabas*

The Judaizers may not have attracted much attention in the church or city of Antioch. Undoubtedly, however, some members were disturbed by their teaching. Possibly some of the Jewish believers were exercised over the matter, but more probably concern was shown by devout Gentile believers who had not complied with Mosaic requirement.

Paul and Barnabas upon their return to Antioch took their stand on this question without a moment's delay or quibbling. They had been led by the Holy Spirit in their work among the Gentiles. The divine blessing had rested upon their labors. The new churches had thrived under their ministry. They knew that ceremonialism would hinder and destroy the progress of Christianity. Nothing would be a greater hindrance to the missionary enterprise.

The debate seems to have enlisted the Judaizers on the one side and Paul and Barnabas on the other. The local leaders at Antioch appear not to have participated very actively. But the congregation was evidently concerned deeply over the "dissension and questioning" which was taking place with such vigor, not to say vehemence.

It is all but certain that the people of Antioch agreed to the position taken by Paul and Barnabas. And yet the visiting Judaizers were such staunch advocates of their historic faith and so representative, as they claimed, of the apostles who had been with Jesus, that it was not thought fraternal to dismiss them summarily with an implied reprimand. Why not refer the question to the mother church at Jerusalem from which these teachers claimed to have come?

4. *Referred to the Apostles and Elders*

It may have been that Paul at first opposed the suggestion, and agreed only after he had received a special revelation (Gal. 2:2). It may be that he then suggested and favored the idea. The reference to Jerusalem was not a recognition of ecclesiastical authority, but a request for fraternal opinion. The church at Antioch had not asked the opinion of Jerusalem when the Holy Spirit ordered the sending out of Paul and Barnabas as missionaries. Yet it was well for two great churches like that of Jerusalem, with its apostles and elders, and that at Antioch, with its missionary prophets and teachers, to stand together on a matter so fundamental as the present problem. At all events, a fraternal discussion was much to be desired and might do much good.

So it was that by vote or other formal arrangement in their assembly the brethren appointed Paul and Barnabas and certain other brethren, including perhaps Titus and possibly Luke, as messengers to the church at Jerusalem. And so they were to appear before the apostles and the elders, who were eminent for piety, wisdom, and efficiency. Surely they could clarify if not solve the knotty question!

5. *Messengers on the Way*

Most likely the Judaizers who had been at Antioch left for Jerusalem earlier than Paul and Barnabas and the other messengers. At all events, the journey was not made with the contending parties in one company.

According to their own hearts' inclination and by beautiful Oriental custom, a group from the church membership in Antioch accompanied the messengers a little way on their journey. Perhaps several went along for a day or two at least.

The route which they followed on their journey of three

hundred miles was apparently down the coast as far as Ptole-
mais and thence across the plain of Esdraelon and south
through Samaria.

It appears that both in Phoenicia skirting the coast and
in Samaria occupying the central part of the country there
were groups of believers organized into small but flourishing
churches. At every point as they proceeded, Paul and Barnabas and the other messengers told their story to enthusiastic
and appreciative crowds. In particular they emphasized "the
conversion of the Gentiles," thus not only elaborating the particular point at issue, but also magnifying the grace of God
which, without distinction, was available to everybody everywhere. To the credit of the Christians along their itinerary,
the messages of the missionaries and messengers "caused
great joy unto all the brethren." Indeed, who of true heart
does not rejoice at the widening horizon and the brightening
prospect!

6. *Reception in Jerusalem*

At length the long journey, which possibly was taken afoot,
was over. The little company reached Jerusalem, which now
was not only radiant with many precious memories, but also a
radiating point for Christianity. At once the little company
must have made known their errand. The first public meeting was therefore arranged, and the messengers were "received of the church and the apostles and the elders." Quickly
the word had passed from house to house and group to group.
Together the church with its leaders, and evidently a large
number of its members, gathered in their accustomed place
of meeting.

The fame of the missionaries had already reached the
Christians of Jerusalem, and they were anxious to see and
hear those who had made such a powerful impact upon the
pagan world. Moreover, they could not have been unacquainted with the disturbance which had arisen recently in

Antioch. Everybody must have been on the alert, therefore, when to the assembled throng Paul and Barnabas "rehearsed all things that God had done with them." Whatever the attitude toward the missionaries and their open-door policy for the Gentiles, the Jerusalem saints were anxious to see and to hear Paul and Barnabas.

7. *Opposition by Christian Pharisees*

In all likelihood several hours were occupied in the reception given by the church at Jerusalem to the returned missionaries, Paul and Barnabas. Both of them must have spoken at length, and it is quite likely that they held themselves in readiness to answer any number of questions propounded from the floor.

At any rate, there rose up out of the crowd "certain of the sect of the Pharisees who believed." This is the only mention made in the Bible of believing Pharisees. We understand that they were believers in Christ and at the same time retained their connection with the sect of the Pharisees.

The position which these Christian Pharisees took openly and in the midst of the services is summarized in a single sentence: "It is needful to circumcise them, and to charge them to keep the law of Moses." Much as they may have rejoiced with the congregation as a whole in the reported conversions of both Jews and Gentiles, these believing Pharisees were yet so devoted to the Mosaic law—and the ceremonial part of it at the moment even more than the moral part of it—that they insisted upon the necessity of conforming strictly to the Jewish ritual. They did not, or perhaps would not, recognize the fact that ceremonialism, having been fulfilled in Christ, was superseded by faith and certainly has no essential relation to salvation.

We imagine that the opposition of these Christian Pharisees, while showing deep conviction and great earnestness, was offered in a respectful and fraternal manner.

It appears likely that Paul and Barnabas, in advance of the formal meeting of the council, held private interviews with Peter, James, and John and some other leaders at Jerusalem.

II. THE COUNCIL

1. *The High Personnel*

The entire church must have been profoundly interested in the burning problem of the hour. And yet the two outstanding official groups in the church were first designated to give their careful consideration to the matter. The apostles had spent years with the great Teacher himself. And since his ascension they had received the Holy Spirit and had done their work under his guidance and with his power, achieving large success.

The elders of the church were evidently its leading men who had risen to positions of prominence by virtue of their purity of character and varied contact with ecclesiastical and civil life, their ripe experience, and their great wisdom.

So, while everybody may have been welcome to the hearing, we may think of the apostles and elders as occupying seats on the platform while the missionaries and others interested in the discussion stood or sat nearby, and other auditors were assembled around them.

When was there ever and where was there ever a more impressive group of men assembled to consider a question so important and so far-reaching in its effects?

2. *The Tense Discussion*

Whether or not the moderator or some other leader brought forward the question to be considered, it was soon before the assembly. Apparently the first thing on the program was the raising of all sorts of objections on the one side or the other. So widespread was the interest that there was "much questioning." It would seem that there were many participants, though, of course, certain ones may have been more prolific than others in presenting difficulties. The discussion was perhaps not angry, but certainly it was earnest. How long it continued we are not told, but plenty of time must have been allowed, and there was no effort to shut off debate.

3. *The Argument of Peter*

When the discussion from the floor had been concluded, Peter arose and delivered an address which marks his last appearance recorded in the book of Acts. First of all, he related his experience in the matter of Cornelius, some twelve or fifteen years previously. Everybody in the company knew that God had chosen Peter in the trance at Joppa to preach the gospel to the Gentile centurion at Caesarea. They knew that Peter had finally obeyed the call and fulfilled his ministry, witnessing in the descent of the Holy Spirit upon the household of Cornelius a Gentile Pentecost. Peter was convinced that God made no distinction between Jew and Gentile, "cleansing their hearts by faith," and not by ceremonies or any other works whatsoever.

Coming to the problem now under consideration, Peter, on the background of his own experience inquired, "Why make ye trial of God?" Had not God expressed his will very definitely concerning this matter? Why then call for new tests? Would it not be presumptuous? Moreover, it was Peter's opinion that to add to Christian duty the burden of Jewish legalism would be to impose a yoke upon the disciples "which neither our fathers nor we were able to bear."

In conclusion Peter expressed his doctrine of salvation: "We shall be saved through the grace of the Lord Jesus, in like manner as they." The Jew has no advantage over the Gentile; the Gentile has no handicap as compared with the Jew in the matter of salvation. All are saved on exactly the same terms and under the same condition. It is for one and all "through the grace of the Lord Jesus."

4. *The Report of Barnabas and Paul*

At the close of Peter's address, the "multitude kept silence" as they came to the next item on the program. The church at Jerusalem had known Barnabas for many years. He had been a member of the church there and one of its leaders. Some of his relatives were still resident in the metropolis and of course identified with the church. He had given largely out of his private resources to care for the poor of the church. He was recognized as a speaker of great gifts and particularly an exhorter of unusual powers. Here at least, his name must stand ahead of that of his illustrious associate, Paul, whom indeed he had sponsored upon the latter's return from Arabia and Damascus.

The two missionaries now rehearsed the "signs and wonders God had wrought among the Gentiles through them." They must have told of twice-born men in Antioch of Syria. They reported the conversion of Sergius Paulus, the proconsul in Cyprus. They gave an account of the thrilling experiences of their missionary tour to Antioch in Pisidia, Iconium, Lystra, Derbe, and other points in the highlands of the Asiatic west.

Think of hearing Barnabas and Paul tell their story to the apostles and elders and the eager throngs that assembled on that historic occasion! If we read with emotion the account on pages that still throb with life, what must it have been to see the veterans rise among their fellows and repeat their incomparable missionary adventures?

5. *The Judgment of James*

When Barnabas and Paul had finished the thrilling story of their missionary journeys, there must have been tense silence throughout the entire room. It was the set moment for the president or moderator of the meeting to deliver his opinion. There was no more distinguished man in the entire group than James. He was the brother of the Lord, but seems not to have accepted him as the Messiah until after the crucifixion. It is thought that Jesus appeared to James (1 Cor. 15:7) at his conversion. He was the author of the Epistle of James and a recognized leader among the saints at Jerusalem.

In his summation of the case, James called attention to how Peter (or Symeon, as he called him by his familiar Jewish name) had "rehearsed how first God visited the Gentiles." No one could mistake the meaning of that outstanding incident, which showed beyond question that the gospel must be given to the Gentiles.

In the next place, James quoted from Amos 9:11-12, showing that the true kingdom will be restored to the true Israel; that the fallen "tabernacle of David" will be repaired; and that God is visiting the Gentiles "to take out of them a people for his name." Thus the experience of Peter and the prophecy of Amos "agree" or symphonize. The figure suggests a circle of musicians, each playing an independent and exquisite melody, and all the melodies together producing a magnificent harmony.

Thereupon James announced his own opinion. First, he would not trouble them who from the Gentiles turned to God. That is, let them be admitted to fellowship in the churches without submitting to Jewish ritual.

However, in the second place, James counseled that a letter be written which would be understood, not as a system of moral procedure, but as a basis of harmony between two groups of conscientious Christians. He felt that "if Jewish exclusiveness had to give way, it was only just that Gentile lawlessness and coarseness should be curbed." In the interest of purity as related to the heathen, he urged that Gentile believers abstain from pollution of idols and from fornication; and in the interest of peace as related to the Jews, he urged that they abstain from things strangled and from blood, both of which were abhorrent to the Jewish mind. Disregard of these matters would interfere very seriously with social fellowship in churches composed of Gentile and Jewish members. Since synagogues were scattered in the great centers of the Roman Empire, and since the law of Moses was preached and read in the synagogues every sabbath, it was highly important that in the interest of peace every cause for sensitiveness or friction should be removed.

The speech of James must have been impressively delivered and certainly its content claimed the rapt attention of everyone present.

III. THE DECISION

1. *The Vote of the Church*

The judgment of James carried great weight. The address of Peter was quite conclusive. The missionaries' experiences told by Barnabas and Paul were thrilling. The questions raised on the floor seemed to have been satisfactorily answered. What then would be the final voice and vote?

The exact formality is not stated, but evidently it was a definite action taken, whether separately or together, by the apostles and by the elders "with the whole church." The decision was thus unanimous.

And yet the decision was not reached simply by debate. There must have been much prayer preceding and perhaps during the session of the council. James certainly made his appeal to the Scriptures. Moreover, the letter which conveyed the decision expressly recognized the leadership of the Holy Spirit.

2. *The Messengers from Jerusalem*

As the church at Antioch had sent messengers to the church at Jerusalem, so now the Jerusalem congregation decided to reciprocate by sending messengers to accompany Paul and Barnabas on their return to Antioch. Two men were designated for the mission. One was Judas called Barsabbas, of whom nothing further is known than what is recorded here, namely that he was a prophet and that he was one of the chief men among the brethren in the mother church at Jerusalem. Some have thought that he may have been the brother of Joseph Barsabbas (Acts 1:23) who was mentioned as successor to Judas Iscariot.

The other messenger was Silas (or Silvanus), who later accompanied Paul on his second tour and assisted in his missionary labors. He also was one of the "chief men" at Jerusalem. In later years he further proved himself worthy of the esteem of his brethren.

3. *The Letter to Gentile Churches*

In a brief letter of only 109 words (157 in the King James Version) the momentous decision of the Jerusalem council was conveyed. It opened with greetings from the apostles, elders, and brethren at Jerusalem. It was addressed to Gentile Christians in Antioch, Syria, and Cilicia—the territory especially infected by Judaistic teaching. It disclaimed the giving of any commandment by the apostles at Jerusalem regarding circumcision or any other matter to the self-appointed Judaizing teachers, and it expressed regret that these teachers had subverted or unsettled the souls of Gentile Christians. It declared that the decision had been reached with entire accord. It stated that the messengers bearing the letter would in person confirm its contents. It bore honest tribute to "our beloved Barnabas and Paul, men that have hazarded their lives for the name of our Lord Jesus Christ."

The heart of the message, which Judas and Silas were to carry and confirm, expressed confidence that it was the will of the Holy Spirit as well as the opinion of the apostles and elders that they would lay upon Gentile Christians no greater

burden than abstinence from four things: (1) from things
sacrificed to idols, including not only outright idolatry, but
the eating of meats whether at public feasts or in homes that
set such meats before their guests, thus countenancing
idolatry; (2) from blood, which pagans sometimes drank
(occasionally with wine) or cooked, but which was forbidden the Jews, who regarded it as representing life; (3) from
things strangled or killed without draining off the blood,
which also was forbidden the Jews and for the same reason;
and (4) from fornication, which may have included not only
unchastity, which was common among the Gentiles at the
time, but also a prohibition of the intermarriages which were
contrary to Jewish law.

"From which if ye keep yourselves, it shall be well with
you." Abstinence for the sake of others is a great Christian
principle, and no one can maintain high fellowship without
adherence to the precepts of morality. As to the decision of
the council, Robertson points out that there is the spirit of
concession here and love, but no compromise of principle.

4. *The Presentation at Antioch*

There was perhaps a formal religious service, dismissing
the distinguished missionaries and the special delegates as
they turned their faces northward. It may be that some members of the Jerusalem church accompanied them part of the
way. At any rate, after a journey of about three hundred
miles they came back to Antioch in Syria. At once "having
gathered the multitude together, they delivered the epistle."
Everybody was eager to know what had been done in Jerusalem.

The letter was read to the congregation. The reader's name
is not given, but we may well think that the reading was
very emphatic and impressive. Indeed, the public reading
of the Scriptures to this day constitutes an outstanding fea-

ture of every worship service. Not unlikely there was public comment on the contents of the letter as soon as it had been read. Both Judas and Silas must have addressed the crowd. Undoubtedly Barnabas and Paul made their report. Others who were present in Jerusalem at the council may have been called upon to add their impressions of the council and their understanding of the decision.

The membership of the Antioch church, upon hearing the letter and the comments upon it, "rejoiced for the consolation." The light of a new day was now dawning upon them. They must gird themselves anew for world conquest in the name of Christ.

IV. Leaders in the New Day

1. *Judas and Silas*

The messengers from Jerusalem to Antioch sustained their reputation of being chief men and prophets. They exhorted the brethren in the Syrian metropolis. They confirmed them in their faith and forward look. They spent some time on their mission. They did not exhibit unseemly haste, and certainly they were welcome among their brethren of the north. At length they were "dismissed in peace," probably in an affecting farewell service. So they returned "unto those that had sent them forth."

It appears that Silas went to Jerusalem for only a short stay, and that he soon came back to Antioch, since shortly thereafter he accompanied Paul on his second missionary journey.

2. *Paul and Barnabas*

The two great missionaries remained in Antioch for some weeks or months. They resumed their ministry of teaching and preaching the word of the Lord. They associated with themselves many other capable workers. Thus a great missionary church was spiritually prepared for further outreach into the Roman world.

FOR CLASS ACTIVITIES AND FURTHER STUDY

Question-Answer Study

Who were the Judaizers? What caused some of them to go from Jerusalem to Antioch? Who sent them? What was the result of their visit? What was the occasion of the Jerusalem council? How was it composed? What authority did it have? Were its deliberations democratic or autocratic? What spirit was manifested by both parties to the controversy? What was the point of Peter's testimony before the apostles and elders? When the entire congregation reassembled, what statement did Barnabas and Paul make? On the merits of the issue, what opinion did James suggest? What concession to the contenders did he recommend? Were James' recommendations authoritative, or final? How were the findings of the council to be communicated to the church at Antioch? Analyze the letter sent from the standpoint of its preamble, its purpose, its contents. How was the letter received? Who continued the teaching and preaching of the word in Antioch?

Suggested Topics for Assignment-Report Conference

Judaism Versus Christianity
Genesis of the Jerusalem Conference
The Sessions of the Conference
James' Wise Words
The Committee and the Letter
The Work Continued at Antioch
The Plan of Salvation
Church Differences and How to Settle Them

Research Activities

1. The council at Jerusalem illustrates many elements which should characterize the business meeting of a Baptist church. In the account in Acts 15 find evidences of (1) Christian love, (2) freedom of discussion, (3) acceptance of the Scriptures as the guide for polity, (4) agreement reached through dependence on

the Holy Spirit, (5) democracy in decision, (6) concern for the whole program of the Lord's work.

2. Read Paul's letter to the Galatians, marking the passages in which it is evident that Paul is refuting the teachings of the Judaizers—which teachings were making inroads into the churches in Galatia.

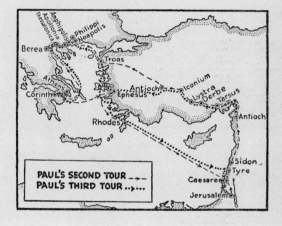

PAUL'S SECOND TOUR --→--
PAUL'S THIRD TOUR ..→...

CHAPTER 5

5

PAUL

Beginning 2nd Journey. (handwritten)

IN MACEDONIA

Acts 15:36 to 17:15

ANXIOUS TO RENEW his labors in Asia Minor and beyond, Paul made this proposition to Barnabas, who had been his companion on the first tour: "Let us return now and visit the brethren in every city wherein we proclaimed the word of the Lord, and see how they fare."

I. SECOND TOUR OF ASIA MINOR

1. *Expansion: the Workers*

Barnabas agreed, but he was bent on again taking with them his kinsman, John Mark, of Jerusalem. To this plan Paul did not agree, since Mark had turned back from Perga when they were on the threshold of their work in Pamphylia, Pisidia, and Lycaonia.

So sharp did their contention become over the matter that Paul and Barnabas agreed to separate, the understanding apparently being that Barnabas would revisit his native country of Cyprus, while Paul would revisit the countries west of his native Cilicia. At any rate, instead of one company, there were now two—Barnabas attended by Mark sailing for Cyprus, and Paul attended by Silas proceeding through Syria and Cilicia. Thus the force was doubled, and the work of missions went on.

2. *Edification: the Churches*

Before Paul retraced his tour in Asia Minor, he spent some time in Syria in the neighborhood of Antioch and then toured through Cilicia, the scene of an earlier but unrecorded ministry.

His special work now was "confirming the churches" by encouragement, indoctrination, and doubtless exhibition of the letter from the Jerusalem council touching the Christian liberty of Gentile believers.

Taking the main road through Cilicia from Tarsus or thereabouts, Paul soon found himself at Derbe, whence after a brief stay he passed on to Lystra. Here occurred another important phase of missionary work.

3. *Enlistment: Timothy*

A trophy of the former visit to Lystra was a young man by the name of Timothy, who was the son of a Greek father and a Jewish-Christian mother of exceptional piety. So well had Timothy, after his conversion, wrought in the spread of the gospel that Paul now found him in high repute among the brethren of both Lystra and Iconium.

Needing just such an assistant in his work, Paul wished Timothy to accompany him, which he gladly did. In order to forestall possible complications that might arise in dealing with the Jews, Paul thought it wise to have Timothy submit to the Jewish rite of circumcision.

So they went on their way, establishing the churches in the faith and daily witnessing accessions to the number of the believers as the gospel for all races was proclaimed in all its power.

4. *Evangelism: the Holy Spirit*

Under guidance of the Spirit, Paul and his companions visited new fields in Asia Minor, though some which they planned to enter were closed to them. Thus they traversed Phrygia and also spent some time in Galatia, where Paul, evidently detained by an unknown malady longer than he had planned, was cordially received by the Galatians and did a remarkable work among them.

The Holy Spirit forbade the missionaries to carry out their proposed evangelism in the Roman province of Asia and would not permit them to enter the province of Bithynia. Moreover, they passed by the province of Mysia without attempting to evangelize it.

But notwithstanding these providential restraints, the work of Christian missions was widening throughout Asia Minor, so that there was a great work behind Paul as well as a great task before him when he reached the city of Troas (near the ancient Troy) on the shores of the Aegean Sea.

II. CALL TO EUROPE

1. *The Vision at Troas*

At Troas, Paul had the good fortune to add another valuable member to his missionary party. It may have been without prearrangement, or, more likely, at the request of Paul, who was possibly still emaciated from his sickness in Galatia, that Luke, the beloved physician, became henceforth the attendant, associate, and chronicler of the great apostle.

The question of questions before Paul at Troas was the field for his future labors. However, he was not long kept in suspense. Before him at night in a vision there stood a Macedonian, beseeching him to come to that country: "Come over into Macedonia, and help us."

Thus the path of duty was made clear, and Paul determined to pursue it without a moment's delay.

2. *The Voyage to Philippi*

Heeding his call to a new continent, the apostle to the Gentiles took the next boat from Troas to a European port. They sailed to the island of Samothrace, which they reached in a day, and there anchored for the night. The next day they reached the city of Neapolis, which was an important harbor on the Macedonian coast. Landing here, they set foot for the first time on the soil of Europe.

And now began a work which in coming centuries was to make this favored continent a lighthouse for the rest of the race. As Paul and his companions went from city to city, the seed of gospel truth was sown; converts were won; churches sprang up; workers were enlisted and equipped for efficient Christian service. It is an interesting story of beginnings in a region which for intellectual brilliancy and spiritual darkness, political strength and moral weakness, was unsurpassed elsewhere in the world.

From Neapolis, a journey of ten miles inland (though they might have sailed up the Gangas River) brought the missionaries to the city of Philippi, which as a Roman colony was not only a military center but also in its government a miniature of the Imperial City on the banks of the Tiber.

III. FOUNDING OF THE PHILIPPIAN CHURCH

1. *Meeting by the Riverside*

Though the Jews were not numerous enough in Philippi to have a synagogue there, a place of prayer by the riverside beyond the city limits was maintained, principally, as it appears, by a few devout women. Thither the missionaries went on the sabbath and seized the opportunity to preach the gospel. They spoke with conviction, and they brought good news. Undoubtedly they were heard with rapt attention and appreciation. Good seed was being broadcast in ready and fertile, even though virgin, soil.

2. Conversion of Lydia

One of the eager listeners was Lydia, a local dealer in dyed goods, which were doubtless imported from her native city of Thyatira. The words of Paul went straight to her heart, which the Lord opened. She believed and thus became the first known convert in Europe. And she showed her faith by being baptized, by leading her household (family or business, or both) to believe and be baptized, and by constraining the missionaries to be her guests during their stay in the city. Thus, the Philippian church was founded.

3. Support of the Missionaries

It is worthy of special note that Paul and his associates were able to fulfil their ministry in Philippi without drawing on their private resources or supporting themselves by manual labor, as they were not above doing and certainly did when necessary.

Liberality was characteristic of the Philippian saints, who not only showed their devotion to Paul once and again, but also made their contribution in money and men to the cause of Christian missions.

IV. PERSECUTION AT PHILIPPI

1. The Occasion: the Damsel

A slave girl fortuneteller, who was actually a demoniac, though her ravings were shrewdly turned into cash, was owned by a stock company in Philippi. They advertised her as inspired by Apollo with power to give oracular direction and to reveal the future. On many successive days she followed the missionaries, bearing true yet undesirable testimony to their character and mission. Weirdly she shouted: "These men are servants of the Most High God, who proclaim unto you the way of salvation."

Finally Paul, as unwilling that his ministry should be associated with soothsaying as he was indignant that moneylovers should make capital out of this poor girl's plight, turned and commanded the evil spirit in the name of Jesus Christ to come out of her. The demon obeyed the same hour, and the girl thus relieved and restored was no longer serviceable and subject to her masters.

2. *The Outrage: Scourge and Stocks*

When the evil spirit was cast out of the soothsaying damsel, her owners, realizing their gains were gone, determined upon revenge. Hence, stirring up a mob, they seized and dragged Paul and Silas before the city authorities, accused the missionaries of being troublesome Jews teaching unlawful customs among the Romans, and had the satisfaction of seeing them unmercifully whipped by the lictors, without the required formality of a trial, and roughly cast into prison, where they were confined in the noxious inner cell, with the additional and needless indignity and torture of having their feet made fast in the stocks.

3. *The Opportunity: the Jailer*

Though rudely scourged and shut in a stenchful dungeon, with their wounds undressed and their wrenched legs in the torturing stocks, Paul and Silas were not dejected. They prayed so fervently and effectually that their prayers burst forth in trusting, joyous song, attracting the attention of the other prisoners. Then came the miraculous earthquake, moving the prison foundations, throwing open every door of the building, and shaking the shackles from the person of every prisoner.

Aroused from slumber and seeing the prison doors all open,

the jailer drew his sword to kill himself, since he knew his life would be forfeited by the escape of the prisoners intrusted to his keeping. But Paul prevented the jailer's suicide by declaring every prisoner in his place.

Then came the transition from mental alarm to spiritual conviction. The man who was on the verge of self-murder was now seeking salvation. The jailer called for a light, sprang into the prison, fell trembling before the missionaries, brought them out from the inner cell to the prison court, and inquired what he must do to be saved. The answer of Paul and Silas to his awakened, inquiring soul is a classic and a model: "Believe on the Lord Jesus, and thou shalt be saved."

They at once followed up the terse requirement of faith in Christ by explaining further the word of the Lord to the entire household. That they all believed in Christ is evident; for they were immediately baptized in the prison pool or nearby river. The jailer quickly revealed his new nature, for he washed and mollified the stripes made by the cruel scourge; he brought the missionaries into his own personal apartments, where food was served them; and he and his household experienced the joy of faith and service.

4. *The Outcome: Release and Fellowship*

At daybreak the lictors who had scourged Paul and Silas came with word for their release from the magistrates, who may have been conscience-smitten over the matter, or at least thought it had gone far enough.

But Paul declined to go forth as an escaping criminal. He sent word to the magistrates that he and Silas, being Roman citizens and having been punished without trial, would not leave prison except under the personal escort of the magistrates themselves. The fact that the prisoners were Roman citizens was a thunderbolt to the authorities, whose conduct exposed them to arraignment and possible execution. They were glad enough, therefore, to come to prison and bring out

Paul and Silas as free men in the public eye, however, requesting them to relieve the situation by departing from the
city.

The missionaries complied, but not until after they had
visited the house of Lydia, met and cheered the brethren,
and left Luke and Timothy for a time, with a view to building up the infant church.

V. MINISTRY AT THESSALONICA

1. *Arrival from Philippi*

From Philippi, Paul and Silas pursued their way westward
over the great Roman highway known as Via Egnatia. A journey of thirty-three miles brought them to the city of Amphip-
olis, situated on the Strymon River near its mouth. Traveling
thirty miles farther, they reached the city of Apollonia,
through which they passed and went on thirty-seven miles
beyond to their objective point, Thessalonica, the metropolis
of Macedonia, situated at the head of the Thermaic Gulf,
and a hundred miles overland from Philippi.

2. *Three Sabbaths in the Synagogue*

As Paul was accustomed, he began his ministry in the local
synagogue of the Jews. On three successive sabbaths he reasoned with them out of the Scriptures that the Christ there
foretold must suffer and be raised from the dead and that
Jesus whom he was preaching unto them, having fulfilled
these conditions, was the Christ of the ancient and accepted
prophecy. As a result, some of the Jews believed and attached
themselves to the missionaries, as also did a great number of
Greek proselytes, and not a few leading women of the city.
A church was thus organized, and it was a splendid beginning of Christian work in a great city. To this church Paul
later addressed the first of his epistles.

3. *The Jealousy of the Jews*

But the cause was not to prosper without persecution. The unbelieving Jews in their jealousy employed a gang of conscienceless street loafers to form the nucleus of a mob, which was quickly gathered and with great uproar centered upon the house of Jason, the host of Paul and Silas, whom they expected to maltreat and possibly murder.

4. *The Assault on the House of Jason*

Not finding the missionaries there, the mob dragged Jason before the city authorities and noisily shouted the charge: "These that have turned the world upside down are come hither also; whom Jason hath received: and these all act contrary to the decrees of Caesar, saying that there is another king, one Jesus." Though the people and their rulers were concerned over the charge thus made, nothing was done except to require security from Jason, who was doubtless a respected and well-to-do citizen, and from his companion, whereupon they were released.

5. *The Departure of Paul and Silas*

In view of the popular excitement, it was impossible for Paul and Silas to do further work in Thessalonica at that time. Therefore, the brethren sent them away that night on their journey to another and readier field of labor.

VI. MINISTRY AT BEROEA

1. *Services in the Synagogue*

A trip of sixty miles brought Paul and Silas to the city of Beroea (Berea), which was beautifully situated on the eastern side of Mount Olympus overlooking the Haliacmon Valley. Here they found the Jews numerous enough to have a synagogue, and it was in the synagogue that as usual the missionaries began their work, since here were those who believed in the one true God and accepted the Scriptures as his Word.

2. *Nobility of the Bereans*

The Bereans surpassed the Thessalonians in their hearty reception of the apostolic message, which, however, they tested for themselves by a daily study of the Scriptures. As a result of the faithful preaching of Paul and Silas and of the revival in Bible study, either to verify or to falsify their message, there were many professions of faith among the Jews. Among the converts there were also several Greek women of distinction and not a few men.

3. *Troublers from Thessalonica*

When the news reached Thessalonica that Paul and Silas were at work in Beroea and having success there, a delegation of Thessalonian Jews came to Beroea and stirred up the people with a view to counteracting the work of the missionaries. While not inciting the violence shown at either Thessalonica or Philippi, they were, nevertheless, successful in their opposition, culminating as it did in the departure of Paul.

VII. ARRIVAL IN ATHENS

The anti-Christian feeling aroused at Beroea was evidently directed chiefly against Paul. Hence the Berean brethren sent him with an escort thirty or forty miles to the coast and thence by sea two hundred miles to Athens.

Meantime, Silas and Timothy were left at Beroea to build up the church there, until the brethren who had accompanied Paul to Athens returned with word from the apostle that they should speedily join him in that city.

FOR CLASS ACTIVITIES AND FURTHER STUDY

Question-Answer Study

Who suggested the second missionary journey, and for what purpose? Why did Barnabas and Paul part company? Who became Paul's traveling companions? What do we know of the young man from Lystra whom Paul chose? Explain the circumstances that turned Paul toward Europe. What is the significance for us that the gospel came to Europe? Tell what you can of the history of Philippi. So far as the record goes, who was the first convert to Christianity in Europe? Was she a European? How were the missionaries entertained for the first part of their visit in Philippi? What miracle did Paul perform in Philippi? Why did this miracle offend some of the "best people" in the city? What opposition did they stir up against the missionaries? How were Paul and Barnabas treated? Tell of their experiences in the jail at Philippi. Trace Paul's course from Philippi to Athens.

Suggested Topics for Assignment-Report Conference

Paul's Traveling Companions
The Missionaries and Lydia
The Missionaries Arrested and Imprisoned
Transformation of a Jailer's Household
Honorable Departure from Philippi
The Journey to Athens

Research Activities

Review the account of Paul's first missionary journey, listing the places he visited. Indicate by an X if a church was established at the place. Check the places Paul revisited on the first journey.

As you continue with the accounts of Paul's second and third journeys, complete the list of places visited and churches established. Every time you find Paul revisiting a church, write against the name in your list the reference or references which tell of his visit. Mark the churches in your list to which Paul addressed one or more epistles. What conclusion would you draw from this study in regard to the importance Paul attached to developing strong churches?

CHAPTER 6

I. ACTIVITIES IN ATHENS

  1. Waiting for Fellow Workers
  2. Stirred by Idolatry
  3. Reasoning in the Synagogue
  4. Disputing in the Market Place
  5. Encountered by the Philosophers
  6. Getting Athenian Reactions
  7. Brought unto the Areopagus

II. ADDRESS TO THE AREOPAGUS

  1. The Scene
  2. A Masterpiece
  3. The Introduction
  4. The Content

III. ATTITUDE OF THE ATHENIANS

  1. Indifference
  2. Curiosity
  3. Scorn
  4. Indecision
  5. Faith

IV. ATTITUDE OF THE APOSTLE

  1. To the Council
  2. To the City

V. MINISTRY AT CORINTH

  1. Settlement
  2. Beginnings
  3. Enlargement
  4. Success
  5. Vindication

VI. THE RETURN TO SYRIA

6

*Continuing 2nd journey
took 3 yrs.*

PAUL

IN ATHENS AND
CORINTH

Acts 17:16 to 18:22

THE ADDRESS OF PAUL on Mars Hill in the heart of Athens was the feature of his stay there, which lasted at most only a few weeks and was less resultful apparently than his labors at any other point in all his vast missionary journeys.

I. ACTIVITIES IN ATHENS

1. *Waiting for Fellow Workers*

The apostle had left some of his associates in Thessalonica when he left that city so abruptly under the lash of persecution. Some scholars have thought that Paul went to Athens more to find a place of retreat than for the purpose of including that city in the sphere of his work. Others have thought that "he may have wished to play the part in Athens that Philo did in Alexandria." [1] At any rate, the apostle paused for a time in the educational center of the Roman Empire which, though its golden age had been gone four

---

[1] Gore, Goudge, Gullaume, *New Commentary on Holy Scriptures* (New York: The Macmillan Co., 1928), III, p. 365. Used by permission of publisher.

centuries, was still the artistic and intellectual center of the world.

Paul was waiting in Athens for some of his fellow workers to come to him, for he was very lonely (1 Thess. 3:1). At length Timothy and Silas did come to the apostle's side, but both were probably sent back to the Macedonian cities and churches with instructions to rejoin him later at Corinth.

2. *Stirred by Idolatry*

Naturally one would be stirred with high emotion in such a city at such a time. But Paul seems not to have been stirred by the illustrious history of Athens, which was the city of Pericles and Demosthenes, Socrates and Plato and Aristotle, Sophocles and Euripides. He was not stirred by the culture and philosophy of the city, which has been described as "a huge decadent university." Indeed, there had been a sad decline, for "philosophy had degenerated into sophistry, art into dilettanteism, oratory into rhetoric, poetry into verse-making."[2] Nor was Paul keenly responsive to the splendid works of art which adorned the city, and made it famous throughout the world to this day. "His spirit was stirred to its depths to see the city completely steeped in idolatry" (Acts 17:16 Williams).

As a Jew and as a Christian, Paul would revolt at every representation of God in material form. He was making another contact with polytheism. For Athens, according to Pausanias, contained more statues than all the rest of Greece. According to Pliny, there were three thousand public statues in the city at the time of Nero. Petronius started the witticism that it was easier to find a god than a man in Athens. Undoubtedly the city was full of idols, and at their sight it is

[2] James Stalker, *Life of St. Paul* (Westwood, N. J.: Fleming H. Revell Co., 1912), p. 96.

no wonder that Paul's spirit "was stirred within him, when he saw the city wholly given to idolatry."

3. Reasoning in the Synagogue

According to his custom, Paul began his work in the local synagogue. It may have been that the apostle did simultaneous work among both Jews and Greeks, spending the sabbath in the synagogue and other days in the market place. At any rate, he reasoned with the Jews and those who worshiped with them, doubtless preaching his familiar doctrine that Jesus was the Messiah. We are not told whether Paul was welcome in the synagogue or was heard coldly. It is possible that Stephanas, whose household was "the firstfruits of Achaia" (1 Cor. 16:15), was converted in the synagogue services in Athens, though his name is associated with the church at Corinth.

But the main thing about the apostle's work in Athens was not its contact with Judaism, but with paganism.

4. Disputing in the Market Place

As Socrates had done five hundred years before on the same spot, Paul began conversations every day in the market place with those who met him. The Agora was the public square and recognized as an intellectual exchange or "the lounge of the learned." Here "Socrates had taught, here was the Academy of Plato, the Lyceum of Aristotle, the Porch of Zeno, the Garden of Epicurus." We may well suppose that in his argument with all who paused to question him, Paul attacked idolatry, atheism, and materialism. A new voice was thus raised, and it had the accent of authority.

5. Encountered by the Philosophers

There were two great rival philosophies of the day held by educated Athenians. "Stoicism was the philosophy of the majority of serious-minded people. Epicureanism that of the frivolous and irreligious."[3]

The Epicureans were named after their founder, Epicurus (341–270 B.C.). They believed that the happiness of mankind was most effectively promoted by striving for pleasure, by which was meant bodily and mental states free from pain. They did not commend unreservedly the lower kinds of pleasure. They had no faith in Divine Providence, but held that the world was under the power of chance. The Stoics believed that human happiness was best attained by the practice of virtue as indicated by the law of nature. They believed also in Divine Providence, but only as superintending in a general way the structure of the world, leaving the individual to the subordinate operation of unalterable natural laws.[4]

As to the estimate of these two philosophies it has been said:

Stoicism is the noblest creed devised by man without the aid of special revelation. . . . Some of the moral utterances of Stoic teachers such as Epictetus, Marcus Aurelius and Seneca have never been surpassed. . . . Epicureanism was valuable as a protest against fatalism; man *could* control his life. It delivered many from base superstitions, and in its best forms, such as we see it in Lucretius, excites our reluctant admiration. But it was atheistic in tendency and peculiarly liable to be abused by mean-souled men.[5]

As these "Pharisees and Sadducees" of Athens, as Josephus called them, encountered the apostle, we discover their relationship to the gospel. Always it conflicts with the two ruling principles in man's nature, pleasure and pride. These were the principles set forth by the Epicureans on the one hand and the Stoics on the other.

In Epicureanism it was man's sensual nature which arrayed

[3] J. R. Dummelow, *A Commentary on the Holy Bible* (New York: The Macmillan Co., 1930), p. 842.

[4] *Teachers' Testament* (New York: Thomas Nelson and Sons, 1912), p. 330.

[5] Gore, Goudge, Guillaume, *op.cit.*, pp. 25, 26.

itself against the claims of the gospel; in Stoicism it was his self-righteousness of intellect.[6]

It is easy to understand why the Epicureans and the Stoics fell into conflict with Paul. Their contrasting philosophies were both in direct opposition with Christianity.

6. Getting Athenian Reactions

The appearance of Paul in the Agora aroused much interest in Athens, and there were some who called him a babbler or an idle prater or gatherer of words and phrases. As Williams translates: "Some said, 'What is this scraps-of-truth-picker trying to say?'" (Acts 17:18). They compared Paul to a man hanging around in the markets picking up scraps of food that fell from the carts, implying that he was a plagiarist who picked up scraps of wisdom from others.

Others who heard Paul declared that the apostle was a seeker after novelty because he set forth strange gods. Evidently he magnified Jesus as God, but they may have misunderstood his reference to the resurrction, which they took to be the name of another deity.

> Some took Paul's reference to *Jesus* (a masculine noun) and to the *resurrection* (in the Greek a feminine noun, *anastasis*) to mean that he was preaching a male and female deity, respectively.[7]

7. Brought unto the Areopagus

The interest was so great or the curiosity so intense that Paul was brought unto the Areopagus. He was not violently taken, nor was he on trial like Socrates, but under escort came before the upper Athenian council, which was the

[6] Horatio B. Hackett, *Commentary on the Acts of the Apostles* (Philadelphia: The American Baptist Publication Society, 1885), p. 278.

[7] Ernest W. Burch, *The Abingdon Bible Commentary* (Nashville: Abingdon Press, 1929), p. 1119.

governing power of the city. Every member of it was over sixty years of age and had occupied some important office of state. They had jurisdiction in criminal and political cases as well as those affecting public morals. They must have had some censorship over lecturers and may have been ready to examine Paul with respect to the doctrine he was declaring in the market place. If the court was not sitting at the time, as some think, the place of meeting was available for the discussion, and some members of the court certainly were present. Whether the place of meeting was on the summit of Mars Hill or somewhere down its slope is uncertain, though tradition points out the seats on the summit occupied by the council.

When Paul appeared before that august tribunal, or a company of the greatest intellects of Athens, the philosophers in deferential sarcasm made inquiry, "May we know what this new teaching is, which is spoken by thee?" They realized that he was bringing to their attention certain strange things, that is, things which to them were surprising or shocking. Yet the Athenian inquisitiveness was equal to the occasion. "Now all the Athenians and foreign visitors in Athens used to spend their time in nothing else than telling or listening to the latest new thing out" (Acts 17:21 Williams). Paul, therefore, had his audience and his Athenian opportunity.

II. ADDRESS TO THE AREOPAGUS

1. *The Scene*

As Paul stood in the midst of Mars Hill, he was in full view of the city of Athens. Below him was the temple of the Eumenides. To the east was the Acropolis fronting him and the Parthenon rising above him. On his left was the great bronze statue of Minerva, the champion of Athens, and on his right the temple of Victory. Behind him rose the temple of the Attic hero, Theseus. Below him were a multitude of smaller temples and altars.

We are reminded of Moses on Sinai where he received the tables of stone, and of Elijah on Mount Carmel when his altar was consumed with heavenly fire, and of Jesus on the Horns of Hattin when he delivered the Sermon on the Mount. Paul's sermon at Athens was a marker in the line of approach which the gospel makes to the culture of the world.

2. A Masterpiece

From the standpoint of oratory, the address delivered by Paul was "a masterpiece of real eloquence on the greatest of themes" (Robertson), an address that "in courtesy, adroitness, philosophy, logic, polish and power is one of the masterpieces of oratory." [8]

The address was also a masterpiece in its message.

[It was] a commendation of the gospel to the hungry heart of heathendom. . . . Just as in the synagogue of Pisidian Antioch he had sought to conciliate the Jews by an historical review, proving that the Gospel was the consummation of their ancestral faith, so now in the Court of the Areiopagus he seeks to commend it to the Greeks by proving it the fulfilment of their age-long yearning after God.[9]

3. The Introduction

As Peter stood in the midst of the Sanhedrin, so Paul faced the court of the Areopagus, and in the same words used by Demosthenes in his orations, Paul began: "Ye men of Athens," or "Gentlemen of Athens."

His first comment was a courteous reference to their re-

[8] James H. Snowden, *Snowden's Sunday School Lessons* (New York: The Macmillan Co., 1933), p. 374. Used by permission of R. R. Snowden, copyright owner.

[9] David Smith, *The Life and Letters of St. Paul* (New York: Harper and Bros.), pp. 145, 147.

ligiosity or carefulness in religion. Actually the Athenians were proud of this distinction. Xenophon had written of Athens as "all altar, all sacrifice and offering to the gods." Paul therefore stated a truth, and at the same time caught attention, when he declared the Athenians were extremely reverential.

In his strolls about the city Paul had been inspecting their sacred institutions and observing the objects of their worship. He thus referred not only to statues but to altars and temples. Doubtless he appreciated their art, but could not approve the works of art that were consecrated to paganism.

However, among their objects of worship the apostle had discovered an altar bearing the inscription, *Agnosto Theo*, "To An Unknown God" or "To the God Whose Name Is Not Known." It has been thought that this altar had been erected during a plague, when the people had tried and failed to find some god to help them. It had, of course, a pagan meaning, but was capable of higher interpretation.

Here then Paul found his point of contact. The unknown God can be known. As Williams translates: "It is about the Being whom you are in ignorance already worshiping that I am telling you" (Acts 17:23). Paul therefore set out to satisfy the longing of the heathen heart for the true and living God. "He unfolded the great truths of the unity of God and the unity of man which lie at the foundation of Christianity." [10]

4. *The Content*

In the synagogue Paul stressed the messiahship of Jesus. But before the Areopagus his principal topic was "The Living God." The address, totaling only two hundred and fifty words, was a masterful exposition of God's place and power in human history. It may be outlined as follows:

[10] Stalker, *op.cit.*, p. 97

2

T.	3500.00
L.	3450.00
B.	2800.00
C.	3000.00
H.	2800.00
K. base)	15550.00
	2400.00
3000.00	
	9550.00

15555.00
4.00
2

$$5)\,\overline{3000}\,(600$$
30
4
00

3500.
3450
2800
3000
2800
2400
17950

DOCTRINE OF GOD

1. God is Creator. This doctrine was new to the Greeks, for their gods were not creators but supervisors.
2. God is Lord. Think of his sovereignty, his spirituality, his self-sufficiency.
3. God is Benefactor. He is not dependent on men for anything whatsoever; it is he who gives to all life and breath and all things.

DOCTRINE OF MAN

1. Man was made by God's power. "He made of one every nation of men."
2. Man dwells on God's earth.
3. Man is governed by God's will. God has determined the appointed seasons for the nations, that is, the stages in their history.
4. Man is intended for God's glory.
5. Men are dependent on God's mercy. "In him we live, and move, and have our being."

DOCTRINE OF SALVATION

1. Men are saved by a living God.
2. Men are saved by an overlooking God. "The times of ignorance . . . God overlooked"; that is, he overlooked the times when they knew no better.
3. Men are saved by a commanding God. "Now he commandeth men that they should all everywhere repent."

DOCTRINE OF ACCOUNTABILITY

1. Why? "Inasmuch" as God is sovereign and man is subject and the way of salvation is open; men are responsible.
2. When? "He hath appointed a day."
3. Who? "He will judge the world in righteousness."
4. By whom? "By the man whom he hath ordained." The name of Jesus was not given at this point, having been given again and again in the Agora, and no doubt was to have been given later in Paul's address.

DOCTRINE OF ASSURANCE

1. There is assurance in the divine Christ.

2. There is assurance before the judging Christ.
3. There is assurance through the available Christ.
4. There is assurance by the guaranteed Christ. "In that he hath raised him from the dead."

Very explicitly Paul declared the resurrection of a dead man, and he gave it as the divine guarantee of Christ to all men. Such a statement had absolutely no parallel in any teaching which the philosophers had ever heard. Socrates had, on that very spot, proclaimed the immortality of the soul, but the resurrection of the body was a new idea to the Greek philosophies who heard Paul. The statement that there had already been a literal resurrection of the body of Jesus was more than they would accept.

It was at this point apparently that there was an outburst of surprise, mingled perhaps with scorn, followed by clamor and crowding together so that the sermon was never finished. The address so far had been only a skilful prelude to the proclamation of the Christian message.

> It only remained, in order to complete his [Paul's] well-known circle of thought on such occasions, that he should have set forth the claims of Christ as the object of religious hope and confidence, that he should have exhorted them to call on his name and be saved.[11]

III. ATTITUDE OF THE ATHENIANS

1. *Indifference*

The Athenian attitude toward the apostle and his message was distinctly different from that he had experienced thus far in Europe, whether at Philippi, Thessalonica, or Beroea. Instead of scourge and stocks, he had met the highest indifference that ever chilled a religious enthusiast. Moreover, "this cold disdain cut him more deeply than the stones of the

[11] Hackett, *op.cit.*, p. 284.

mob or the lictors' rods." [12] It was not even the formality of a decision, if the proceedings were legal. The meeting simply broke up in confusion. "The case was laughed out of court, and he was set at liberty." [13]

2. *Curiosity*

As the council melted informally off Mars Hill, and the philosophers chatting lightly together went their way, there were some who marveled at it all. They wondered if this strange doctrine had after all a grain of truth in it. Their Athenian inquisitiveness did not forsake them. Some were ready to hear still more.

3. *Scorn*

"Some mocked," or sneered. They mocked not at a philosophical argument for resurrection in the abstract, but at the declaration of Paul that God had actually raised one person from the dead. They aimed their shafts of sarcasm at a testimony rather than a tenet. "The doctrine of the resurrection was repugnant alike to the Epicureans, who disbelieved a future life altogether; and to the Stoics, who held that human souls would be reabsorbed into Deity." [14] The physical resurrection of Jesus from the dead is still the subject of ironical remark. But it is true despite cynical bitterness.

4. *Indecision*

Others said, "We will hear thee concerning this yet again." Were they serious? If so, there is no record that they later asked the apostle to give them another opportunity. Were they showing Attic courtesy or waving Paul aside with an idle compliment? Was their request an opiate to their con-

[12] Stalker, *op.cit.*, p. 98.
[13] Smith, *op.cit.*, p. 147.
[14] C. H. Irwin, *Irwin's Bible Commentary* (The John C. Winston Co., 1928), p. 462.

sciences? Did they, like Felix, fear to hear more? Alas, that a more convenient season seems never to have come!

5. *Faith*

The apostle had sown the good seed in the flintiest soil on the globe. But even on the limestone ledges of Mars Hill he did not scatter the gospel seed in vain. "Some men, however, joined him and came to believe" (Acts 17:34 Williams). The most prominent was Dionysius, a member of the court (said to be composed at that time of twelve judges) and of course a most highly respected citizen of Athens, having been archon (chief magistrate) of the city. Tradition says that he became the first bishop of Athens and died a martyr.

Another convert was a woman named Damaris. Some scholars claim that she must have been an educated courtesan, but she may well have been an aristocratic woman. It is not expressly stated that she was of the high class of the women converted under Paul's ministry in Thessalonica and Beroea. At any rate, the grace of God reached her heart, and her name lives on imperishable pages.

It appears that Paul was probably never without at least one convert wherever he went. However, no church seems to have been founded at Athens at this time.

IV. ATTITUDE OF THE APOSTLE

1. *To the Council*

As Jesus withdrew from Gadara after working a thrilling miracle, so Paul withdrew from Athens after preaching a wonderful sermon. The language would imply that his departure was abrupt. We cannot think of him as going down from Mars Hill in a rage, but he must have been deeply disappointed at the treatment he received. Highly educated as he was, he had been heard with appreciation by the mercantile populations of other cities. Normally he might have felt more at home among the polished Athenians than elsewhere in the world. But their culture would make no room for Christ, and so there was nothing for the apostle of Christ to do but to withdraw. And when Paul turned his back upon the illustrious court and descended from Mars Hill, a greater than Socrates went his way.

2. *To the City*

"After these things he [Paul] departed from Athens." His entire stay was evidently brief, but he must have left Athens almost immediately after his address on Mars Hill. He visited Greece later, but there is no mention of a stop at Athens. He wrote no letter to Athens, so far as we know. He said nothing in his letters about Athens and his experiences there. He sent no messages to converts in the city. He delegated none of his associates to go there. He left the city abruptly and absolutely.

Was Paul's work in Athens a failure? One writer speaks of it as "Paul's only missionary failure." Another says: "It is a sad story—the noblest of ancient cities and the noblest man of history—and he never cared to look on it again." From such a view we dissent decidedly. The last verse of the record embodies a story that thrills to this day. The conversion of Dionysius and Damaris was worth every effort the apostle himself could make to win them to Christ. What must have been the unrecorded influence of that address on those who heard it, and through them upon the Greek and Roman world! And who, as Paul delivered the address, could foresee that the pagan Parthenon should ere long become a Christian church? Moreover, out of that address, light is yet permeating the whole earth. Paul's work in Athens, far from being a dismal failure, was a glorious success. His labor was not in vain in the Lord.

V. MINISTRY AT CORINTH

1. *Settlement*

A great field was furnished the apostle in Corinth, famous for its wealth and power from the time of Homer. It was situated on the narrow isthmus connecting Peloponnesus and northern Greece. With two famous harbors it held the land traffic from north to south and received by sea rich merchandise from the chief ports of Europe and Asia. This most corrupt and effeminate city in Greece contained a heterogeneous population of some four hundred thousand. There were a great many Jews here who had been expelled from Rome by the Emperor Claudius. To this number belonged a native of the district of Pontus in Asia Minor, Aquila, and his wife, Priscilla, who followed the trade of tentmaking. When they were compelled to leave Rome, they came to Corinth and began business. When Paul, who had been trained in the same occupation, reached Corinth, he formed a partnership with Aquila, and for some time supported himself by manual labor.

2. *Beginnings*

A good start was made by Paul in the synagogue, where he spent every sabbath and spoke convincingly to both Jews and Greeks on his favorite theme that Jesus is the Messiah. But his work went on under extreme difficulty; he was sick in body, depressed in spirit, confronted with poverty, and lonely in work. When, however, Silas and Timothy rejoined him, bringing good news and a contribution from the churches in Macedonia—whither he had sent them on a special mission—Paul devoted himself wholly and enthusiastically to his ministry. First of all, he energetically addressed the Jews, maintaining that Jesus is the Christ. But they met his earnestness with blasphemy, his argument with abuse, and his compassion with hatred.

3. *Enlargement*

A growing work was actually developed by the organized, determined hostility of the Jews. Instead of narrowing, it widened the ministry of the missionaries. Shaking his raiment in token that he was shaking off all responsibility for their conduct, Paul said to them that their blood was upon their own heads, that he was clear of blame, and that he would extend his ministry to the Gentiles. Immediately he left the synagogue and made his preaching headquarters in an adjoining building owned by Justus, who no doubt became a Christian. It was a decisive step to take, and one that drew the line sharply between believers and unbelievers. But Paul knew what he was about, and he was successful in winning many converts to Christ.

4. *Success*

A gracious ministry ensued. Even the chief ruler of the synagogue, Crispus, with all his house, believed on the Lord, and he was one of the few baptized by Paul (1 Cor. 1:14). Besides this remarkable family, many other Corinthians also believed and were baptized. Though these first fruits were encouraging, yet the apostle was frequently depressed by the difficulty of the work in a heathen metropolis, by the hardness of heart shown by the Chosen People, and by the fear that he would be martyred in the midst of his labors. He was evidently in a state of despondency when the Lord in a night vision calmed his fears, designated his duty, assured him of divine protection, and promised a great ingathering at Corinth. Thus encouraged, Paul prolonged his ministry there for eighteen months, proclaiming the gospel in that notoriously wicked center of commerce.

5. *Vindication*

While Paul was at Corinth, and perhaps two or three months before the close of his ministry there, Gallio, a brother of the philosopher, Seneca, was made proconsul of Achaia, with headquarters at Corinth. Taking advantage of Gallio's well-known, even-tempered, and uniform courtesy, the enemies of Paul had the apostle arraigned before the proconsul under the charge: "This man persuadeth men to worship God contrary to the law," referring not to Roman but Jewish law. When Paul was about to speak in his own defense, Gallio told his accusers that if it were a matter of crime he would hear the case, but since he considered it a quibble over words and names and religious law, he would be no judge of such matters. Thereupon, he drove them from his presence. Before they could get beyond the proconsul's hearing, the Jews who sought to destroy Paul were themselves attacked by the Greeks, Sosthenes the chief ruler of the synagogue being flogged right under the eyes of Gallio, who showed no concern over the matter, probably feeling that the tumultuous Jews got what they deserved.

For some time Paul tarried still at Corinth, building up the church there, planting other churches in the province, training workers, and writing to the Thessalonians the earliest of his epistles.

VI. THE RETURN TO SYRIA

After completing a ministry of eighteen months at Corinth and having his head shaved at Cenchrea (ten miles from Corinth) in fulfilment of a vow, the nature of which is unknown to us, Paul set sail for Syria. He was accompanied by Aquila and Priscilla as far as Ephesus, which they probably reached in a fortnight.

The voyage across the Aegean Sea between the two great merchantile cities of Corinth and Ephesus was made with frequency. The fortnight which it took for Paul to make the trip was about the average time consumed. The vessel on which Paul sailed seems to have been bound for Syria and to have stopped only a short time in the harbor at Ephesus. Here Aquila and Priscilla remained, while Paul continued his journey. However, during his brief visit at Ephesus Paul used every opportunity to preach. He "entered into the synagogue, and reasoned with the Jews" (Acts 18:19).

Paul spoke with such acceptability that the Jews desired him to remain some time with them. Unable to comply with the request because he must hasten on to Jerusalem in time to observe the approaching feast—probably Pentecost—he promised to return later, if providentially permitted. Sailing from Ephesus, he landed at Caesarea, and thence went overland to Jerusalem. After a short stay, during which he attended the feast and paid his respects to the church, Paul returned to Antioch in Syria, having been absent on his second missionary journey about three years.

This second missionary journey had involved an expansion and further working out of Paul's ministry as the one of whom the Lord had said, "He is a chosen vessel unto me, to bear my name before the Gentiles" (Acts 9:15). On his first journey Paul's program of work was to follow, insofar as he could, the pattern set forth in his words to the Jews as recorded in Acts 13:46: "It was necessary that the word of God should first have been spoken to you: but seeing ye put it from you, and judge yourselves unworthy of everlasting life, lo, we turn to the Gentiles."

The council at Jerusalem seems to have increased Paul's emphasis on his ministry to the Gentiles. Note the very positive statement of Acts 18:6 as he broke with the Jews in Corinth. Never did Paul lessen in his "heart's desire and prayer to God for Israel . . . , that they might be saved" (Rom. 10:1), but increasingly he magnified his calling as the apostle to the Gentiles. The last words of Paul recorded in Acts are those spoken to the Jews in Rome: "Be it known therefore unto you, that the salvation of God is sent unto the Gentiles, and that they will hear it" (Acts 28:28).

FOR CLASS ACTIVITIES AND FURTHER STUDY

Question-Answer Study

Sketch briefly the history of Athens. From what point did Paul come to Athens? For whom did he wait? What was the most obvious sin of Athens? How did the sight of this sin affect Paul? Where did Paul argue with the citizens? In your own words, define Epicureanism and Stoicism. What was the attitude of the philosophers toward Paul? Define Areopagus. Quote the introduction of Paul in his speech on Mars Hill. Outline Paul's address. What destroyed the interest of Paul's hearers? What were the immediate, visible results of the message? Is there any necessary connection between culture and salvation? Did the quality of Paul's audiences make any change in Paul's message?

Why did Paul come to Corinth? What friends did he make upon arrival? How did he spend the sabbath? What open breach did Paul have with the Jews? What arrangements did he make for private instruction? Who were among his converts? What message did the Lord bring to Paul in a vision? How long did Paul remain in Corinth? Who was Gallio? What came of the effort of the Jews to prosecute Paul before Gallio? What rather undignified performance took place when Gallio dismissed the case? What conditions in Corinth made Paul's work exceedingly difficult?

Suggested Topics for Assignment-Report Conference

History of Athens
Idolatry in Athens
The Lonely Missionary
The Areopagus
Inquisitive and Argumentative Athenians
Paul's Mars Hill Address
The Effect of the Address
The Real Significance of the Statue to an Unknown God
Human Hunger for God
The Universal Message

Research Activities

In the book of Acts we have the account or at least the main theme of several of Paul's sermons. Note, for example, Acts 9:20, 22; 13:16–41; 17:2–3; 18:4–6. How does the sermon recorded in Acts 17:22–34 differ in pattern from Paul's usual procedure? How do you account for the difference?

CHAPTER 7

7

PAUL

IN EPHESUS AND
OTHER FIELDS

Acts 18:18 to 20:38

PAUL'S THIRD MISSIONARY JOURNEY (about A.D. 54 to 58) was characterized chiefly by his three years' ministry at Ephesus, one of the populous cities of Asia Minor and the seat of worship to the goddess Diana, or Artemis, whose original temple here was one of the famous Seven Wonders of the World.

I. INSTRUCTING JOHN'S DISCIPLES

The apostle's first work at Ephesus was to win to Christ and the church a dozen men who were disciples of John the Baptist. On meeting them, Paul inquired whether they received the Holy Spirit when they believed? They were amazed at the question, for they had not heard of the marvels of the Spirit's coming at Pentecost. They had simply received John's baptism, but since, as Paul told them, John's baptism, was preparatory to the coming Messiah (who had, in fact, already come), and since possibly they had been baptized unto John rather than unto the Christ whom John preached, they now accepted Christ and were baptized "into the name of the Lord Jesus." Moreover, "when Paul had laid his hands upon them, the Holy Spirit came on them; and they spake with tongues, and prophesied."

II. PREACHING IN THE SYNAGOGUE

Following his usual custom, Paul began his regular work in the synagogue of the Jews. Here he spent three months. The burden of his ministry was "the things concerning the kingdom of God." In formal address and in personal argument he convincingly taught the people. There were some who accepted his teaching, but others in their unbelief and hardness of heart rose before the multitude and bitterly denounced Christianity. These opponents were sufficiently influential to convince Paul that the aggressive work which he planned at Ephesus could not be carried on with the synagogue as a base.

III. TEACHING IN THE SCHOOL OF TYRANNUS

Withdrawing with his disciples from the inhospitable synagogue, Paul found a most convenient and strategic meeting place in the schoolroom of Tyrannus, who was evidently a sympathizer and friend, if not a convert and disciple of Paul. Here Paul arranged to have daily meetings for preaching and consultation. Vigorous as the work was, and hard as it was on those who did it, there was no cessation for a period of two whole years. That it was fruitful there is no question.

IV. EVANGELIZING THE PROVINCE OF ASIA

Visitors to Ephesus from nearby cities and villages were attracted to the lecture hall of Tyrannus to hear the apostle, and they scattered his teaching far and wide over that region. Very likely also some of the Ephesians were sent out to evangelize the surrounding country. It is possible that Paul himself went to various cities in the neighborhood and laid the foundations of some of the seven churches of Roman Asia.

At any rate, "all they that dwelt in Asia heard the word of the Lord, both Jews and Greeks."

V. ROUTING THE MAGICIANS

In a city where magic arts were widely practiced and exceedingly popular, it is little wonder that Paul was endowed with miraculous power far surpassing the highest achievements of the heathen magicians. In fact, handkerchiefs and aprons which came in contact with his body were carried by the people and applied to their sick and demoniac friends, effecting wonderful cures and casting out evil spirits.

Thinking that the name of Jesus was simply the magic secret of Paul's wonder works, some strolling Jews, who professed to deliver from the influence of wicked spirits, decided to use it in dealing with cases brought before them. But when the seven sons of Sceva, a Jewish chief priest, tried it, the evil spirit, to their consternation, answered: "Jesus I know, and Paul I know; but who are ye?" Not only so; but "the man in whom the evil spirit was leaped on them, and mastered both of them, and prevailed against them, so that they fled out of that house naked and wounded."

Like wildfire the news of this utter rout spread through the city and, as a result, everybody was filled with awe and magnified the name of Jesus. Many of the magicians believed in Christ, and in making their confession they revealed their deceptive practices and made a public bonfire of their magic books to the value of several thousand dollars. "So mightily grew the word of the Lord and prevailed."

VI. IN TOUCH WITH EUROPE

1. *Writing to the Church at Corinth*

While busily engaged at Ephesus, Paul heard of the dissensions and irregularities in the church at Corinth. He was grieved to hear of the four parties that had sprung up there: a Pauline party, overzealous for him as founder of the church; an Apollonian party, bewitched by the oratory of Apollos; a Petrine party which, claiming Peter as authority, was bent on mixing up Jewish ideals with Christianity; and a Christ party which, in antagonizing the other elements, became itself a faction.

In their distress over the state of the church, some of the members had written Paul asking his counsel and help. He therefore wrote his first letter to the Corinthians, giving requested instruction about marriage, the relation of Christianity to previous circumcision or slavery, meat offered to idols, collections for the poor, spiritual gifts, and church order. He also wrote concerning several vices that had crept into the church: factional strife, lawsuits before heathen judges, inexpedient liberty, licentious indulgence, and abuse of the Lord's Supper. Finally, he asserted his apostolic authority and presented the historical proofs of the resurrection.

2. Sending Messengers to Macedonia

In this connection it is interesting to observe another phase of the far-reaching program, which included distant fields with that in which Paul was laboring. He was planning to revisit the cities of Macedonia and Greece after doing his work at Ephesus, then to make a journey to Jerusalem, and immediately thereafter to realize his long-cherished hope to go to the city of Rome. So now from Ephesus he sent two of his valued attendants, Timothy and Erastus, into Macedonia for the double purpose of strengthening the churches and securing a contribution for the indigent and needy brethren in Judea.

VII. Stirring up the Devotees of Diana

The success of the gospel meant to that extent the failure of idolatry. In consequence of Paul's ministry, therefore, the business of idol making in Ephesus was on the decline. The waning market for silver shrines of Diana was first felt by the silversmiths of the city, and they determined to get Paul out of the way. Their meeting was assembled and addressed by the president of the guild, Demetrius, who shrewdly adverted to the source of their wealth as being paralyzed by Paul whose work tended to make the splendid temple a byword and to rob the great goddess of her glory. The crowd, wildly indignant, shouted, "Great is Diana of the Ephesians!"

Rushing into the streets, they threw the whole city into confusion, laid hands on two of Paul's traveling companions, Gaius and Aristarchus of Macedonia, and crowded into the great amphitheater with a view to crushing out Ephesian Christianity and its apostle. Learning what was going on, Paul started to enter the amphitheater and appear before the people, but he was prevented by the brethren and by some friendly officials who entreated him not to run the risk. Meantime, everything was utter confusion within the amphitheater, for some yelled one thing and some another, while the majority had no idea what drew them together. After a time, the Jews, wishing to clear their skirts of any responsibility that might be attributed to them for what Paul had done, put forward Alexander, one of their number, to address the mob; but when they saw that he was a Jew, the uproar broke out afresh and for two hours like madmen the multitude cried, "Great is Diana of the Ephesians!"

Finally the townclerk of Ephesus quieted the mob and obtained a hearing. His address was both sensible and successful. He asserted the loyalty of the Ephesians to their goddess, which nobody questioned, and therefore they should not be excited about it. The men who had been dragged into the amphitheater were not arraigned as temple robbers nor even as blasphemers of Diana; if against them Demetrius and his fellow craftsmen had any definite charge, let them take the matter to the courts and settle it legally there. And if the people were interested in other matters, they had their appeal in the regular assembly. Such a causeless concourse and uproar as this was sure to endanger Ephesian rights and liberties if brought to the attention of the authorities at Rome. "And when he had thus spoken, he dismissed the assembly." So the crowd was calmed and dispersed without striking the blow intended for Paul.

VIII. Revisiting Former Fields

1. *Macedonia*

The uproar at Ephesus hastened but did not change the apostle's plan to visit the European churches which he had founded on his second tour. Immediately following the outbreak at Ephesus, Paul assembled the disciples, bade them an affectionate adieu, and set out for Macedonia. He seems to have been accompanied by Tychicus and Trophimus. On their way they stopped for a time at Troas, where they preached the word. Crossing over the sea, they came to Philippi where Timothy and Titus, the latter with much-desired intelligence direct from Corinth, joined Paul, and all were pleased with the progress made by the Philippian brotherhood. While here the apostle again took up his pen.

Paul's first letter to the Corinthians, as he learned through Titus, had a salutary effect, though there was still a factious minority which depreciated the apostle's authority, misrepresented his motives, and censured his conduct. Under the strong and mingled emotions caused by such intelligence, the second letter to Corinth was immediately written. It was designed to carry forward the work of reformation, to caution against false teachers, and to prepare the Corinthians for the writer's approaching visit. A collection was solicited for the poor in Judea, and the apostle defended himself against the calumnies of his critics. Such was the message which Paul sent to Corinth from Philippi at the hands of Titus, Trophimus, and Luke.

2. *Illyricum*

Traversing Macedonia, the apostle no doubt revisited Thessalonica, Beroea, and other points. But he seems to have entered new fields at this time; for in a letter written a few months later, he says that "from Jerusalem, and round about even unto Illyricum"—the province stretching northward from Greece bordering on the Adriatic Sea—"I have fully preached the gospel of Christ" (Rom. 15:19). He does not tell us the success that attended his efforts, but it was a period of seed-sowing if not of harvest.

3. *Corinth*

Very likely the winter had set in when Paul, having completed his mission in Macedonia, Illyricum, and northern Greece, and feeling assured of the readiness of the brethren to receive him, came again to Corinth, where he spent three months. Of his stay little is told us, but he doubtless silenced his enemies and edified the church. Also two letters were written, and, on the eve of his departure, there was another outbreak of Jewish hostility.

4. *Letter to the Romans*

The apostle was naturally very anxious to promulgate Christian doctrine at Rome, which was the great receiving and distributing center of the world. Already he had planned to make a visit there, after carrying to Jerusalem the poor fund collected from the churches of Greece and Macedonia. Before leaving Corinth for Jerusalem and probably at the hands of Phoebe, a deaconess of the church at Cenchrea, who just now going to Rome could carry the letter direct to its destination, Paul wrote and forwarded his letter to the Romans. His purpose was to supply the lack of needed personal teaching, to pave the way for his intended visit, and to prepare the church to aid him in the proposed mission to Spain. In its two great parts—the doctrinal section dealing chiefly with justification and sanctification by faith, and the ethical section embracing an exposition of many practical affairs— the letter to the Romans gives us the fullest and most systematic presentation of the apostle's teaching that we have.

5. *Letter to the Galatians*

The churches in Galatia had been more than once troubled by Judaizing teachers, who seemed to follow in the track of Paul, opposing his apostolic authority, doubting his doctrine, and urging entire obedience to the Jewish ceremonial laws. Learning of the dangers that threatened them, Paul, without his usual amanuensis but with his own hands, wrote his letter to the Galatians. His object was twofold: First, he wrote to repel the insinuation that he was not an apostle, or that he did not stand on an equality with the other apostles; for the establishment of his position was necessary in order to preserve his influence and make permanent his work among the churches. Second, he wrote to expose the Judaistic and other errors which had crept into the churches and deceived the thoughtless Galatians; hence he established the doctrine of justification by faith and so demolished the position of hostile teachers.

6. *On to Troas*

When about to sail from Corinth for Syria, Paul, hearing of a Jewish plot against his life, changed his route and retraced his way overland via Beroea and Thessalonica to Philippi. His traveling companions were Sopater of Beroea, Aristarchus and Secundus of Thessalonica, Gaius of Derbe, Timothy of Lystra, and Tychicus and Trophimus of Roman

Asia. Remaining at Philippi until after Passover, Paul and Luke, after an evidently stormy sail requiring five days instead of less than two to cross that part of the Aegean Sea, reached Troas, whither the other members of the party had preceded them.

Here the apostle remained a week, the feature of the stay being the all-night farewell meeting just before resuming the journey. The meeting was held in a brilliantly lighted upper chamber, which seems to have been the meeting place of the local church. About midnight and while the service was yet going on, a lad by the name of Eutychus fell from the third-story window where he was sitting asleep, and was taken up dead. But Paul went down and fell on the lad and embraced him and restored him to life. Then the group of believers resumed the service, observing the Lord's Supper and having the apostle talk till daybreak, when they were dispersed to their homes, and he pursued his way on foot and alone to Assos, there joining his party aboard ship and sailing uneventfully till they came to the seaport city of Miletus.

7. Meeting the Ephesians at Miletus

Anxious to know the situation at Ephesus and yet aware that if he included that city in his itinerary he would be detained long enough to miss reaching Jerusalem in time for Pentecost, Paul decided to have the elders or bishops of the church at Ephesus meet him at Miletus, a distance of twenty-eight or thirty miles from Ephesus. Accordingly, on reaching Miletus, he sent for them, and they came to him without delay.

The address Paul delivered to the elders was one of the most affecting we have from the lips of the great apostle. He recounted his ministry at Ephesus; his open record and humble heart; his many tears, trials and temptations; his fearless and faithful preaching and work, publicly and privately; his unvarying gospel alike to Jew and Greek: "Repentance toward God, and faith toward our Lord Jesus Christ." Paul then told of the bonds and afflictions before him and of the fact that they should see his face no more. He urged upon them their duty of vigilance and fidelity in view of the unsparing wolves and untrue teachers who would arise among them. Finally, he enjoined upon them special care for the weak, as shown by his own example and by the words of Jesus—not elsewhere recorded—"It is more blessed to give than to receive."

When Paul had finished his address, all knelt in fervent prayer, with the apostle leading them. With streaming eyes and aching hearts, they fell on Paul's neck and kissed him farewell, sorrowing at his word that never on earth should they see him again. "And they brought him on his way unto the ship."

FOR CLASS ACTIVITIES AND FURTHER STUDY

Question-Answer Study

How would Paul reach Ephesus from Athens? Give a very brief statement of the historical importance of Ephesus. Why was Paul's first stay in Ephesus so brief? Who was Apollos? Through his questioning, what distinction did Paul make between followers of John and Christians? Why did Paul move from the synagogue to the school of Tyrannus? Relate the incident of the sons of Sceva. What was the effect of the defeat of these impostors? What was the trouble with Demetrius and his guild? What use was made of the silver shrines? How much did the mob know about the situation? What service did the town clerk render in this connection? What argument against mob law is found in this incident? Sketch on a map Paul's travels from Ephesus to Miletus. What was the purpose of this journey? What meeting was held at Miletus? What was the substance of Paul's message to the elders? Describe the scenes of the farewell between Paul and his friends.

Suggested Topics for Assignment-Report Conference

The City of Ephesus
The Temple of Diana
The Disciples of John and Christians
Paul's Educational Ministry
Paul and the Exorcists
The Great Bonfire
Paul and the Silversmiths
Revenue and Religion
Mob Rule
From Ephesus to Miletus
Paul's Address at Miletus
An Affectionate Farewell
The Conquering Christian

Research Activities

Suppose you had access to no Scripture passages other than the account of Paul's work at Ephesus and his meeting with the Ephesian elders (Acts 18:18 to 20:38). What could you learn from this passage about (1) baptism, (2) the Holy Spirit, (3) evil spirits, (4) justification by faith, (5) responsibilities of church officers, (6) the core of the gospel message?

CHAPTER 8

8

PAUL

IN JERUSALEM AND CAESAREA

Acts 21 to 26

PAUL'S THIRD great missionary journey concluded not at Antioch in Syria, as did the first and second journeys, but at Jerusalem, where he was arrested and later sent as a prisoner first to Caesarea and then to Rome.

I. PAUL IN JERUSALEM

1. *Reception*

When Paul and his companions reached Jerusalem they were cordially welcomed by the church there. The day after their arrival they were given a public recognition and hearing by the assembled elders and church. After exchanging greetings, Paul "rehearsed one by one the things which God had wrought among the Gentiles through his ministry."

It was a story that thrilled and rejoiced many who heard it, but there were also many, doubtless the great majority, who listened coldly to the apostle as he recounted the salvation of the Gentiles who had come into the churches without first becoming Jewish proselytes. In fact, the Judaizing element in the church had been informed that Paul had been teaching "all the Jews who are among the Gentiles to forsake Moses, telling them not to circumcise their children, neither to walk after the customs." The charge was but a half-truth, for the apostle had taught the Jews not to discard Moses but to fulfil his law by accepting the Messiah; nor had he antagonized circumcision and other Jewish customs except as a substitute for salvation through Christ.

It was therefore not at variance with the teaching or practice of Paul that he agreed to the suggestion of James which, without compromise of conviction on his part, would pacify the Jewish zealots who would crowd the city during the feast and become aware of the apostle's presence there. The suggestion was that Paul join with four men, probably members of the local church, in fulfilling their vow by personal abstinence and ceremonial purification, himself bearing the expenses of all five as an example especially meritorious and commendable from a Jewish point of view. James thought that such an act would contradict the damaging report that was current and at the same time show conclusively that Paul himself was an observer of the Jewish law, though, as the council of Jerusalem had decreed, Gentile Christians were free from Jewish ceremonial obligations. Under the circumstances, Paul thought the suggestion a good one and adopted it.

2. *Riot in the Temple*

Almost the entire seven days requisite to the fulfilment of the vow made by the four men, now joined and supported by Paul, were completed when an incident occurred which threw the city into an uproar.

Attending the feast now in progress there were many Jews from Roman Asia, some of whom were doubtless from Ephesus and thus were well acquainted with Paul's work there. They had recognized the apostle on the streets of Jerusalem and observed with him one of their townsmen, Trophimus, who as a Gentile would be denied the Temple privileges which were legal for Jews only. When therefore these visitors from the province of Asia saw in the Temple the apostle and his four companions, they concluded that Paul was profaning the Temple by taking uncircumcised Greeks into its sacred precincts. So they raised the false and cruel shout: "Men of Israel, help: This is the man that teacheth all men everywhere against the people, and the law, and this place; and moreover he brought Greeks also into the temple, and hath defiled this holy place."

Instantly the people ran together from all parts of the Temple and its environs, the tumult increasing every moment. But for their sanctimonious regard for the Temple, the leaders of the mob would have killed Paul on the spot. As it was, they dragged him out and closed the door, expecting to accomplish their murderous purpose in the open street.

3. Rescue by the Captain

For just such an occasion as this Lysias, the captain of the Roman garrison, was prepared. Stationed in the fortress overlooking the Temple area, he immediately learned of the disturbance and with soldiers and centurions rushed upon the scene. The appearance of an armed force quieted the mob, which now stopped beating Paul.

When the captain came up, he arrested Paul, had him double-fettered, and then demanded of the crowd who he was and what he had done. Out of the confused cries the Roman captain could learn nothing, so he started with his prisoner to the castle. So violent and tumultuous were the people, that before they reached their destination the soldiers were compelled to carry the apostle in their arms.

4. Address to the Multitude

When they had reached the castle steps and were about to go within, Paul, using the Greek language, asked the captain, "May I say something unto thee?" The captain was surprised that his prisoner could speak Greek, for he thought him very probably the Egyptian insurrectionist who had terrorized the land as the leader of four thousand wilderness bandits. But when Paul told him he was a Jew and a Cilician, Lysias permitted the apostle to proceed.

Thereupon, facing the multitude, Paul, from the castle steps, beckoned his hand to the people and brought them to a dead silence before him. Then, in the Hebrew language, with which they were acquainted, he delivered his defense. Beginning with the respectful appellation, "Brethren and fathers!" he told of his nativity in Tarsus, his education in Jerusalem, his relentless persecution of Christians, his conversion and baptism at Damascus, his return to Jerusalem with a view of locating there permanently, and his unmistakable call from God, "Depart: for I will send thee forth far hence unto the Gentiles."

To this point Paul was given attention, but the very mention of the word Gentile, threw the mob again into frenzy. Tearing their clothes from them and throwing dust into the air, they shouted at the top of their voices, "Away with such a fellow from the earth: for it is not fit that he should live."

5. *Imprisonment in the Castle*

The captain, being unacquainted with the Hebrew language in which Paul spoke, could only judge of the address by its apparent effects. Concluding that he had a notorious criminal on his hands, he ordered Paul taken inside the barracks and subjected to the ordeal of scourging so that he would reveal his identity and confess the crime he had committed.

But when the soldiers were binding Paul ready for the lash, he asked the superintending centurion if it were lawful to scourge an uncondemned Roman citizen. The centurion, knowing that any officer who did such a thing would forfeit both his position and life, reported the matter at once to the captain, who himself hurried to look into it. To his question Paul declared himself a freeborn Roman citizen, a claim easily verifiable by the records in his case, but if falsely made by any pretender was always punished by death. In this case, the prisoner had been born into civic rights which the captain had been able to secure only by great financial outlay.

The thongs were immediately removed from the body of Paul, and the captain was afraid because he had already gone further than the law allowed in dealing with a Roman citizen under charges before trial. However, he left Paul in chains overnight.

6. Defense Before the Council

In order to ascertain definitely the charges against Paul, the captain summoned the Sanhedrin together and brought the prisoner unbound before them. As the apostle faced the very body to which he had formerly belonged, he must have known personally and perhaps intimately a number of its members. However, his opening sentence claiming that he had lived conscientiously was rudely interrupted by an order from the high priest that a bystander slap him on the mouth. Indignantly Paul resented the blow, saying, "God shall smite thee, thou whited wall: and sittest thou to judge me according to the law, and commandest me to be smitten contrary to the law?" It was a rash utterance, as Paul at once acknowledged, but it was deserved and was prophetic of the assassination of the high priest a few years later.

Unable to make a formal defense that would be effective, Paul took clever advantage of the two parties composing the Sanhedrin by declaring himself a Pharisee on the fundamental question at issue, namely, "the hope and resurrection of the dead." For, while the Pharisees believed in resurrection, the Sadducees hotly denied it, and, in fact, had no room in their faith for either angels or spirits. So when Paul announced his views there was sharp and instant division among the members of the great council. The Pharisees were especially noisy, rising and shouting, "We find no evil in this man: and what if a spirit hath spoken to him, or an angel?" The Sadducees were probably as insistent and vociferous in their outcry against the apostle. In the midst of it all, there was imminent danger that Paul would be pulled to pieces between the contending factions. The Roman captain had therefore to summon his guards and take the prisoner by force from the council chamber.

7. *Promise of the Lord*

With storm after storm of hate bursting in fury upon him, the kingly spirit of the apostle seemed now to droop. But on the very night following his appearance before the Sanhedrin, he was cheered by the presence of the Lord who stood by him and said, "Be of good cheer: for as thou hast testified concerning me at Jerusalem, so must thou bear witness also at Rome."

Confident that he would finally reach the goal of his holy ambition, Paul was ready to face any danger.

8. *Conspiracy of the Jews*

At the dawn of the next day, forty Jews bound themselves together with an oath that they would neither eat nor drink till they had killed Paul. Into the plot they took the chief priests and elders, who were to ask the captain to bring Paul, on the day following, before the Sanhedrin again; and while he was being brought the conspirators were to spring upon him and slay him.

Hearing of the conspiracy, a son of Paul's sister went directly to the castle and told Paul about it. Taken to the captain by one of the centurions at Paul's request, the young man repeated his story of the plot and said that those who were planning it would appear presently to get the captain's promise to bring the prisoner before the Sanhedrin. The captain dismissed his informant under charge of strict secrecy, and determined to send Paul at once to Caesarea, where his case would be heard by Felix, the procurator (or governor) of the province.

At nine o'clock that night the Roman captain sent Paul away on horseback under escort of two centurions, two hundred soldiers, two hundred spearmen, and seventy horsemen, with instructions to bring him safely to Caesarea. Lysias also sent a letter to the governor telling of his connection with the case, how he had rescued Paul who was a Roman citizen, how the appearance before the Sanhedrin had resulted in no charge worthy of bonds or death, and how on discovering the plot against the prisoner's life he had transferred the case to Caesarea. The infantry went with Paul only as far as Antipatris, which they reached the next morning. The horsemen hastened on with Paul and the letter of Lysias until they reached the seat of government and presented both before Felix, who said he would hear the case upon arrival of the apostle's accusers.

II. PAUL AT CAESAREA

For more than two years Paul was detained a prisoner at Caesarea, and during this time he made three notable addresses at court.

1. Trial Before Felix: Indecision

Five days after Paul was brought down to Caesarea from Jerusalem he was followed by the high priest and members of the Sanhedrin who had employed a lawyer named Tertullus to appear before the governor, Felix, against Paul. The speech for the prosecution was a shrewd formulation of the charge that Paul was guilty, first, of sedition among the Jews throughout the world; second, of heresy as a ringleader of the Nazarenes; and third, of profanation of the Temple. The address closed with an assertion that the Jews would have handled the case themselves without troubling the governor, but for the forcible interference of Lysias; still, the governor could examine the prisoner and satisfy himself as to the truth of the charges.

To the speech of their lawyer the Jews gave hearty assent before the governor, declaring it an accurate statement of the facts and doubtless regarding it as an adroit presentation of their side of the case.

The governor beckoned to Paul that his defense was now in order. With a courteous introduction, the apostle began. He denied as totally unproven the charge that he was a mover of sedition; next, he explained his doctrine as embracing many things which his accusers believed and as completing the prophecies which all accepted; and finally he told the story of his alleged profanation of the Temple, which the Asiatic Jews originally making the charge were not here to prove and which was not established before the Sanhedrin. All the charges, therefore, fell to the ground.

The governor saw at once the utter emptiness of the charges brought against Paul. Of course, he should have released the prisoner immediately. However, in deference to the Jews, whose favor he wished to maintain, and doubtless in the hope of securing a bribe from Paul, he deferred the case, declaring he would hear it fully when Lysias could come down to Caesarea. So he kept Paul in custody, though allowing him the liberty of seeing his friends and receiving their ministrations.

Some days after the trial, Felix, in consultation and company with his wife Drusilla, called for Paul, and, as a matter of curiosity, asked him to explain to them his doctrine of Christ. They were expecting something very different from what they heard. Complying with their request, Paul in a message directly pertinent to them, argued for right living and self-control in view of the final judgment. "He reasoned of righteousness, and self-control, and the judgment to come." Righteousness meant justice in its reference to Felix as a public official; self-control was direct in its application to the governor's wicked private life; and the judgment to come will be the time of final and awful account for the deeds done in the body. So personal and so powerful was the plea of Paul that Felix, wincing under it, dismissed the apostle, not discourteously perhaps, but abruptly, saying, "When I have a convenient season, I will call thee unto me."

2. Trial Before Festus: Appeal

Three days after Festus became governor at Caesarea, he went up to Jerusalem. While there, he was importuned by the Jewish authorities to bring Paul to that city for trial, their plan being to waylay and kill him on the way. Festus announced that he would hear the case at Caesarea, whither he went ten days later.

The day after his return, Festus summoned Paul before him and heard his accusers make their unproved charges. The answer of Paul was that he had violated no law, Jewish or Roman. Festus knew that Paul was right and that his accusers were wrong, but in his anxiety to please the Jews he asked Paul if he would be willing to stand trial before him at Jerusalem.

Knowing that his enemies were only trying to compass his death by a ruse, Paul replied that he was being tried by Roman law, that he had done the Jews no wrong, as the governor could clearly see, and that being unworthy of death he was unwilling to be delivered into their murderous hands. Hence, he exercised his right as a Roman citizen, declaring, "I appeal unto Caesar."

After conferring with his council, the governor granted the appeal, and thus the way was open for Paul to go to Rome.

3. *Address Before Agrippa: Vindication*

A few days later, Agrippa II (king of Chalcis by appointment of the emperor, and son of Herod Agrippa I, who had killed James) came with his paramour-sister Bernice on a congratulatory visit to Festus. During the visit Festus told Agrippa about Paul and the status of the case, which embarrassed him as governor since he had no definite charge that would justify sending his prisoner to Rome. Agrippa at once expressed a desire to see and hear Paul, of whom he had no doubt heard much before. Festus arranged for a hearing the next day.

In the great audience chamber at the appointed hour assembled Agrippa and Bernice in royal pomp, the chief military men in their shining armor, and the principal citizens of Caesarea. At the governor's command Paul was brought in and introduced to the assembly as a man whom the Jews wished executed, but being found unworthy of death had been granted appeal to Caesar, though now the trouble was to formulate a statement that would justly bring the case before the emperor at Rome.

When Agrippa gave Paul permission to speak, the apostle, stretching forth his fettered hand, made his memorable defence. After an apt personal allusion to his distinguished auditor, he proceeded to give the story of his life, first as a Pharisee of the strictest type and still holding to the promise made the fathers concerning the resurrection; then, as a bitter persecutor of Christians in Jerusalem and unto distant cities; next as a convert to the Christian faith; and finally as a preacher of repentance among both Jews and Gentiles. On these grounds, declared Paul, the Jews had sought to kill him; but he had continued his testimony, which was nothing else than what was foretold by Moses and the prophets, namely, "How that the Christ must suffer, and how that he first by the resurrection of the dead should proclaim light both to the people and to the Gentiles."

Here the apostle was interrupted by the governor, who thought him mad with much learning because he proclaimed the resurrection. With a courteous reply to the governor, Paul addressed the king as acquainted with the facts given out and the doctrines set forth. But when Paul interrogatively affirmed Agrippa's faith in the prophets, the king replied in jest that Paul would in a little time be actually endeavoring to persuade him to become a Christian; to which in his closing word the apostle rejoined that he devoutly wished, whether in a little or a long time, both Agrippa and the audience were such as he—except the chains.

The regal company then rose up and retired for a conference, in which they agreed that Paul had done nothing worthy of death or of bonds, and Agrippa said to Festus that but for his appeal to Caesar the prisoner might have been set at liberty.

FOR CLASS ACTIVITIES AND FURTHER STUDY

Question-Answer Study

Identify the following characters: Agabus, Mnason, Trophimus, Ananias, Felix, Tertullus, Drusilla, Festus, Agrippa, Bernice.

What concession in the interest of harmony did Paul make in Jerusalem? Upon what evidence did the Jews bring their first charge against Paul in Jerusalem? What saved Paul's life in Jerusalem? How did Paul commend himself to both officials and Jews in his stairway speech? What words of his caused the Jews to fly into a rage? How did Paul divide the Jews among themselves? What encouragement did the Lord bring to Paul? What plot did the Jews form against Paul? Why was Paul taken to Caesarea? Why was he not brought back to Jerusalem for trial? Why was he not released after trials in Caesarea? How many speeches did Paul make in his own defense? Before whom? What was the burden of each of his speeches? How were the judges affected by his speeches? What characteristics did Paul exhibit under fire?

Suggested Topics for Assignment-Report Conference

Paul's Concession to the Jews
Basis of Jews' Attack on Paul
Paul's Stairway Speech
Paul's Debt to the Roman Government
Jewish Conspiracy Against Paul
The Transfer to Caesarea
Paul Before Felix
Paul Before Festus
Festus Presents Paul to Agrippa
Paul Before Agrippa
Some Characteristics of Paul Under Fire

Research Activities

It will be stimulating to study the various trials of Paul recorded in Acts, noting the charges brought against him in each case, and looking for the elements of truth in these charges. To what extent could these true elements be accurately applied to Christians today?

Read Acts 26: 22–23. Using the marginal reference in a teacher's Bible, read passages to show that Moses and the prophets had said "that the Christ must suffer, and how that he first by the resurrection of the dead should proclaim light to the people and to the Gentiles" (Acts 26: 23).

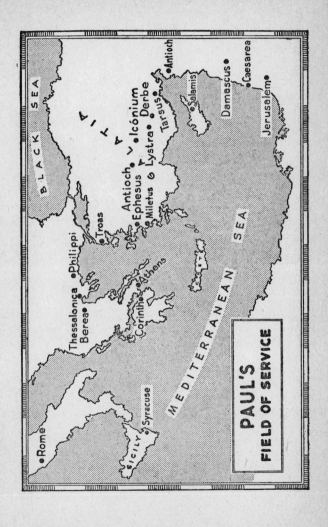

PAUL'S
FIELD OF SERVICE

CHAPTER 9

9

PAUL

IN ROME

Acts 27 and 28

FINALLY Paul realized his hope to preach the gospel in the city of Rome, but stony was the path and stormy the sea that bore him thither.

I. THE VOYAGE

1. *Sailing from Caesarea*

It was about the middle of August, A.D. 59, and only a few days after the hearing before Agrippa that Festus started Paul on the voyage from Caesarea to Rome. The apostle and other prisoners were entrusted to the care of Julius, a centurion belonging to Augustus' band. Luke and Aristarchus accompanied Paul. They sailed in a vessel of Adramyttium bound for ports on the coast of Roman Asia.

After a day's run they reached Sidon, and Paul was allowed to go ashore and visit his friends in the city. Launching thence and encountering contrary winds, they sailed to the north of Cyprus and on to the Lycian city of Myra. Finding here an Alexandrian vessel bound direct for Italy, they went aboard, and after a slow sail of many days they reached Fair Havens on the island of Crete. The stormy season had now arrived, and hence Paul advised that they remain here until it was over. The majority, however, agreed with the shipmaster and the owner in deciding to reach the better Cretan harbor of Phoenix before stopping for the winter.

2. The Wreck at Malta

When a gentle southern breeze sprang up, they sailed from Fair Havens, keeping near the coast and expecting to reach their destination in a few hours. But in a little while a furious northeast wind swept down upon them, rendered the ship helpless, and drove it under the lee of the isle of Cauda (Clauda). During the brief lull they hoisted the small boat aboard, undergirded the ship with cables to strengthen it, and reefed every sail for fear the wind would drive them upon the quicksands off the north African coast. As the tempest continued, the next day they threw a part of the cargo into the sea, and the day following they cast overboard the ship's tackle. For days the clouds hid sun and stars so that the mariners knew not their course, and the hurricane kept up until all hope of rescue was abandoned.

In this dismal hour it was Paul who spoke the word of hope. He declared that the ship would be wrecked but that every man's life would be saved. God had appeared to him promising him that he should see Rome, giving him all his companions aboard the vessel, and showing that they would be cast upon a certain island. On the fourteenth night after the storm struck them, the shipmen, suspecting that they were approaching land, sounded and found it true, whereupon they cast out four anchors and waited for day. The mariners attempted by a ruse to get into a lowered boat and row safely to land, but at Paul's suggestion they were prevented, and the boat was cut loose by the soldiers and dropped into the sea.

Also following Paul's counsel and example, bread and meat

were served the 266 persons on the ship, after which the cargo of wheat was thrown overboard so that the ship could come close to shore. Finally daylight came, and effort was made to thrust the ship into a creek, but the prow was driven fast into the sand, while the stern was being rapidly broken to pieces by the heavy breakers. The soldiers, fearing that the prisoners would swim out and escape, advised that they be killed as the Roman law permitted; but the centurion, determined to save Paul, objected and bade all to cast themselves into the sea and get ashore by swimming or floating on pieces of the ship. "And so it came to pass, that they all escaped safe to land."

On landing, the shipwrecked group learned that they were on the island of Malta. No little kindness was shown them by the islanders, who began by kindling a fire for their comfort, since they were wet and cold. As Paul joined in gathering sticks for the fire, a deadly viper fastened on his hand. When the natives saw it, they concluded that Paul was a notorious criminal who might escape a storm but would certainly be slain by the serpent. But when, unharmed, he shook the reptile from his hand into the flames, they wondered for a while and then concluded that he was a god invulnerable.

For three days Paul and his fellow travelers were entertained hospitably by Publius, the governor of Malta. The courtesy was amply repaid by Paul, who healed the governor's father of a malignant fever and bloody flux and also healed many others throughout the island. Honor and gifts were heaped upon Paul and his attendants when, after a stay of three months, they embarked for Rome.

3. Arriving in the Imperial City

From Malta for Rome, Paul and his party embarked, probably in February, A.D. 60, in a ship of Alexandria which had wintered in the island. Its sign, which was the figurehead carved or painted on the bow giving name of the vessel, was Castor and Pollux, or the Twin Brothers, mythological sons of Jupiter and the votive gods of mariners.

Sailing north eighty miles, they reached Syracuse on the east coast of Sicily, of which it was the capital. Strabo says it was twenty-two miles around the walls of the city and that it rivaled Carthage in wealth. Here three days were spent. The next stop was in Rhegium, a seaport on the southwest point of the Italian coast, where they spent a day. Before the strong south wind which sprang up, they made a northerly run of 180 miles to Puteoli, which it is said they might have made in twenty-six hours. This "Liverpool of Italy" was on the Bay of Naples. Here the voyage terminated, and Paul was permitted to remain a week with the local disciples while the centurion was making arrangements for the land journey before them. Then they proceeded afoot over the highway 140 miles to the Imperial City. To his great joy Paul was met on the way by two parties of the Roman brethren—the first at the Forum of Appius (Appii Forum) forty miles from Rome and the second at Three Taverns thirty miles from Rome.

So Paul came at last to the capital of the Empire, the center of the world's commerce, law, and learning, situated on the seven hills by the river Tiber fifteen miles from the sea.

II. THE FIRST IMPRISONMENT

On arrival at Rome, the prisoners from Palestine were delivered to the prefect of the Praetorian Guard, who had charge of all who were to be tried before the emperor. Paul was not confined in the common prison but was allowed to dwell by himself. This leniency was perhaps attributable to Julius the centurion who had brought Paul from Caesarea. However, the apostle was kept constantly chained to his guardsmen, and since the guards were frequently changed to relieve each other it is evident that many Roman soldiers came under Paul's influence.

1. Interviewing the Jews

When Paul arrived in Rome, very many Jews, some of them wealthy and influential, were residing there. After three days of recuperation from his journey, salutation of the church, and necessary prison preparation, he called the chiefs of the Jews together. This first interview was devoted to an explanation of his appeal to Caesar. Paul's purpose was to set himself right before his countrymen and to win them to Jesus the Messiah. He told them of his groundless arrest, of his virtual acquittal at Caesarea, and of his appeal to Caesar as a measure of self-defense. The real ground of his imprisonment was his misunderstood advocacy of the nation's fondest hopes as now fulfilled in Jesus the Messiah. The Jews responded that they had not heard anything against Paul, though they knew of the hostility toward Christianity. The interview apparently closed with the announcement of another meeting.

Paul's second interview with the Jews was devoted to an endeavor to persuade them concerning Jesus. On the day appointed, the Jews gathered in large numbers at the rented apartments of Paul, or possibly at the more commodious residence of some Roman Christian. The apostle spent the entire day teaching them out of their own Scriptures the things concerning Christ. Evening came and some believed, while others rejected the teaching of the great prisoner. As the members of the audience, some in obstinate unbelief, were leaving the room, Paul quoted the prophecy of Isaiah concerning their hardness of heart, and declared his intention of extending his ministry to the Gentiles. With much heated discussion, the Jews turned away. Apparently, their response included no more than wordiness.

2. *Preaching the Kingdom of God*

During the next two years Paul, though in the charge of, and chained constantly to, a Roman soldier, was allowed to dwell in his own hired house. There he received everybody who came to him, not being permitted to visit the synagogue or go from house to house. In a bold, unforbidden ministry he preached the kingdom of God and taught the messiahship of Jesus.

3. *The Prison Letters*

During his first imprisonment Paul wrote letters to the Ephesians, Philippians, and Colossians, and to Philemon.

The letter to the Ephesians was probably intended as a circular letter to the several churches in the Roman province of Asia, of which Ephesus was the chief city. Hence, it lacks the usual local coloring and is without messages of personal greeting. There is a striking resemblance between the letters to the Ephesians and to the Colossians, which is easily accounted for by the fact that both were written probably within a few hours of each other.

The letter to the Colossians was written after Epaphras, the Colossian pastor, visited Rome with a message of cheer for the apostolic prisoner and a report from his church. This report was in some respects satisfactory to Paul, but the news of incipient error called for immediate attention. Hence, the epistle was sent to refute false doctrine, to warn against wicked teachers, and to establish the Colossians in the faith.

The letter to Philemon, whose house was the meeting place of the Colossian Christians, was called forth by the conversion and return of his slave Onesimus, who after robbing his master, ran away and soon drifted to Rome, where he came up with Paul and was converted. Though Onesimus proved himself serviceable to the apostle, the penitent slave was sent back with this letter to his offended master. He was accompanied by Tychicus, who bore at the same time the letter to the Colossians.

The letter to the Philippians was written in acknowledgment of a timely contribution from the church at Philippi, which was brought by Epaphroditus to Paul during the second year of imprisonment at Rome. After a dangerous illness during his stay, Epaphroditus returned to Philippi bearing this letter of affectionate remembrance.

4. *Hearing Before the Emperor*

After perhaps a little more than two years in custody at Rome, Paul was finally given a hearing before the emperor, and, as he had anticipated, was no doubt set at liberty, although the book of Acts does not give us this record. Though sixty years of age, or older, the apostle apparently laid out a full program of missionary work and was active to the end of his days.

III. Last Tour of the Mission Fields

It is possible that, after his release from his first imprisonment in Rome, Paul went westward on a missionary tour to Spain, as he had earlier hoped. It is not impossible that he visited Britain, as some hold on slight tradition, but the reasons for believing that such a tour was made are not entirely convincing. It is quite likely, however, that Paul revisited his former mission fields and churches in Greece, Macedonia, and the provinces of Asia Minor.

During this period, which was mainly devoted to building up the churches and establishing other missions, the apostle wrote personal letters to Titus and Timothy. The letter to Titus, who had been left in Crete to complete the work Paul had not time to finish, was written by the apostle probably at Ephesus while on the way to Nicopolis to spend the winter. The first letter to Timothy, who seems to have been left at Ephesus, was written by Paul probably during the summer preceding his death.

IV. THE SECOND IMPRISONMENT

1. *Persecution*

Upon the throne of the Roman Empire now sat one of the wickedest monarchs who ever wore a crown or swayed a scepter. And one of the most dastardly deeds attributed to the Emperor Nero was to set the city of Rome on fire for his own amusement and then give Christians the credit for starting the conflagration. Such a persecution as now broke forth upon the followers of Jesus the world has never seen before nor since. They were covered with pitch and burnt as torches, thrown into the arena and devoured by lions, crucified, beheaded. The church at Rome was smitten with an iron hand; its members were ruthlessly slain or sent into exile. And from distant provinces Christians were brought in chains and slaughtered by order of the bloodthirsty emperor.

2. *Martyrdom*

Of course, the great apostle could not hope to escape the cruel mandate of Nero. Soon he was brought to Rome and thrown in a dungeon without his former liberties. At his first arraignment the chief witness against him was Alexander, the coppersmith (2 Tim. 4:14), who may have been the Alexander who tried to address the assembly in Ephesus (Acts 19:33), although we have no proof in the matter.

Back to the dismal cell, without the cloak to warm him in the winter or his books to occupy his mind, Paul was thrust to await the end which he knew was coming. For the last time he took up his pen to write the second letter to Timothy, desiring that his son in the gospel come to him speedily—a desire that was probably gratified. But again Paul was brought before the emperor, and now the sentence of death was passed. Being a Roman citizen, the apostle was not to be crucified or burned, but beheaded. So one spring day— perhaps a bright May morning in the year A.D. 68—the executioners led the prisoner out of his cell and out of the city along the Ostian Road to a convenient spot, where the victim knelt by the block, the gleaming ax did its work, and to the ground rolled the head of Paul, the chief of the apostles and the greatest of missionaries.

FOR CLASS ACTIVITIES AND FURTHER STUDY

Question-Answer Study

Why was Paul going to Rome? Who was his escort? What were the stages of the journey? Enumerate the services that Paul rendered in the storm. How long did they stay on Malta? How were they treated there? What wonders did Paul perform while there? Why were the inhabitants called barbarians? What was the last lap of the sea voyage? How far was it from Puteoli to Rome? What encouragement did Paul meet along the way? How long was Paul a prisoner in Rome? What freedom was given to him? What was his attitude toward the Jews in Rome? How did they receive his message? How did Paul spend his time as a prisoner?

Suggested Topics for Assignment-Report Conference

Handicaps of Ocean Travel in Paul's Day
Paul's Leadership in the Storm
Wintering in the Island of Malta
Paul's Reception and Work in Rome
Paul's Death
Lessons from Paul's Character

Research Activities

A committee may be asked to consult sources available in your church library and find out why many authorities believe Paul was released from his first imprisonment in Rome and later imprisoned and executed.

CHAPTER 10

I. FALL OF THE JEWISH NATION

II. SPREAD OF CHRISTIANITY
1. The Churches in Palestine
2. The Churches in Asia Minor
3. The Churches in the Province of Asia
4. The Churches in the Roman Empire

III. COMPLETION OF THE BIBLE
1. The Gospels
2. The Acts
3. The Pauline Epistles
4. The General Epistles
5. The Revelation

10

RESURVEY

Taking up the story where his Gospel closes, Luke in the Acts of the Apostles traced leading events of the apostolic age through nearly forty years.

The descent of the Holy Spirit on the day of Pentecost was the great beginning. Peter stood forth then and for years afterward as the most commanding figure among Christians.

Scattered from Jerusalem by persecution, the disciples went everywhere preaching the gospel and some Gentiles were admitted to the churches.

After a time Paul appeared and thenceforward occupied foremost place as defender and disseminator of the Christian faith. So successful were his three great missionary tours through western Asia and southern Europe that when he was first imprisoned at Rome (as recorded in the last chapter of Acts) there were vigorous young churches in all the centers of the Roman Empire.

I. Fall of the Jewish Nation

The city which had nailed the Son of man to the cross and mercilessly persecuted the early Christians was itself to be brought low under the mighty hand of Rome.

In the year A.D. 70, Titus, the Roman general, laid siege to the rebellious city of Jerusalem. The horrors that followed are told on some of the best-known pages of history. At last, the Roman eagles were borne in triumph within the city walls and planted amid blood and fire upon the sacred heights. The city was utterly sacked, the Temple with its contents was devoured by the greedy flames, more than a million Jews were slain, and nearly a hundred thousand captives were sold into slavery.

II. SPREAD OF CHRISTIANITY

From other New Testament sources than Acts, we have for that period indirect glimpses of the churches in Palestine and Asia Minor. For the period from Acts to Revelation (which, roundly speaking, was from the destruction of Jerusalem in the year 70 to the close of the first century) we have miniature views of the seven churches in the Roman province of Asia and yet dimmer sidelights upon the other churches throughout the world empire of Rome.

1. *The Churches in Palestine*

Of the groups of disciples in Palestine, the church at Jerusalem holds the center of interest until its apparently complete dispersion at the fall of Jerusalem. The leader of the church, James, who was the Lord's brother, wrote (probably about the year 48) the earliest of the New Testament books, addressing his epistle to the Jewish Christians who were scattered abroad. The epistle to the Hebrews, written about A.D. 69, perhaps in Italy, by one of Paul's associates, if not by the apostle himself, was addressed to a body of Jewish Christians, which may have been the mother church at Jerusalem. Thus from the church in the floodtide of its power the message of James was sent, and to the church on the eve of its own dispersion the epistle to the Hebrews came.

2. *The Churches in Asia Minor*

The planting of Christianity in Asia Minor was due primarily to converts at Pentecost and to the apostle Paul. But others also joined in the blessed work. Peter, for example, seems to have labored in this region. At any rate, he addressed his letters to the saints in the several provinces of Asia Minor, writing either from the literal Babylon on the banks of the Euphrates or from the mystical Babylon (Rome) on the banks of the Tiber. It was evidently a time of great persecution. Peter himself suffered martyrdom, some say at Rome, soon after writing his second letter in A.D. 67 or 68. The Epistle of Jude, brother of James and of the Lord, appeared during this same troublous period and pictures the same general religious conditions. Bitter was the conflict between Caesar and Christ.

3. The Churches in the Province of Asia

Ten or fifteen years passed, and John, the beloved disciple, wrote his epistles at Ephesus, the center of his energetic labors in the Roman province of Asia. Another decade or more passed, and the fiery persecutions under the Emperor Domitian burst forth in their fury. John did not escape. He was sent to Patmos an exile. But on that rocky isle he wrote the great Apocalypse and addressed the churches in the seven cities of Ephesus, Smyrna, Pergamum, Thyatira, Sardis, Philadelphia, and Laodicea. With many professing Christians it was a time of cold love and lax doctrine, but others were sound in faith, abundant in good works, and patient in tribulation.

4. The Churches in the Roman Empire

At the close of the first century, despite difficulties manifold and persecutions dire, churches, aggregating a membership supposed to be at least one hundred thousand, were established in many cities of the Roman Empire—in western Asia from the Euphrates Valley to the Aegean Sea, in northern Africa as far up the Nile as Ethiopia, and in southern Europe from Scythia on the Caspian Sea to Spain.

III. COMPLETION OF THE BIBLE

The twenty-seven books of the New Testament were written by eight disciples of Christ during the latter half of the first century. Fourteen books (if we include Hebrews) were written by Paul; five by John; two each by Luke and Peter; one each by Matthew, Mark, James, and Jude. Very likely seven were written during the decade beginning A.D. 50: James and six of Paul's letters; sixteen in the sixties: the other eight Pauline epistles, the epistles of Peter and Jude, four histories, and the Revelation; and four in the nineties: the Gospel and the epistles of John.

1. *The Gospels*

For our fourfold story of the Messiah we are indebted to Matthew, the publican apostle; Mark, the companion of Peter; Luke, the medical associate of Paul; and John, the disciple whom Jesus loved. By the first of these writers our Lord was presented to the Jews as the Messiah, fulfilling the ancient prophecies; by the second, he was revealed to the Romans as the miracle-working Son of God; by the third, in more systematic treatise, his humanity is emphasized before the Greeks; and in the last, his diety is unfolded before the world. Mark begins with the ministry, Matthew traces back to Abraham, Luke to Adam, and John to the throne of Deity in eternity unbegun. Matthew and Luke dwell on the infancy and childhood of Jesus; John on the early Judean ministry; the three Synoptic Gospels at length on the great Galilean ministry; Luke on the ministry in Perea; all four on the events of Crucifixion Week, followed by the resurrection, appearances, and ascension.

2. *The Acts*

The last of the New Testament histories, far from being a full account of the transactions of the twelve apostles, does not attempt a record of the apostolic body. Little is said of any of them except Peter, and the chief incidents cluster around the apostle to the Gentiles. The book was doubtless written by Luke, for it begins precisely where the Third Gospel closes, and carries forward the history from the ascension in A.D. 30 to the close of Paul's first Roman imprisonment in A.D. 63. Recording the work of the Holy Spirit in the apostolic age, the missionary endeavors of the early churches, and representative discourses of the primitive preachers, the book of Acts is fittingly the sequel to the Gospels and the preface to the Epistles.

3. The Pauline Epistles

Of the thirteen books from the pen of Paul, six may be styled the missionary epistles, because they were written during the period of incessant missionary labors in two continents—1 and 2 Thessalonians, 1 and 2 Corinthians, Romans, and Galatians.

There were four prison epistles—Ephesians, Philippians, Colossians, and Philemon—which were written during Paul's first imprisonment at Rome. Of the three pastoral epistles, 1 Timothy and Titus were written before the apostle's two Roman imprisonments, while 2 Timothy appeared only a little while before the great author was beheaded.

The persons originally addressed by Paul in his letters were scattered over the great centers of the Roman Empire. Thus he wrote to the churches of Galatia and the cities of Ephesus and Colossae in Asia Minor; to Philippi, Thessalonica, and Corinth in the Grecian peninsula; and to Rome the seat and capital of the Empire. He also wrote personal letters to Timothy, his missionary associate; to Titus, his helper in Crete; and to Philemon, his Colossian friend. The letter to the Hebrews, written by an associate or disciple of Paul if not by the apostle himself, was addressed to Jewish Christians, perhaps in Palestine, and was designed to stimulate them to steadfastness amid the taunts and persecutions of their Jewish kinsmen.

4. *The General Epistles*

Of these seven letters, three were written by John, two by Peter, and one each by James and Jude. John was the beloved disciple and apostle, author of the Fourth Gospel and the Revelation, and the only survivor of the twelve during the last decade of the first century. Peter spent his closing days as a foreign missionary, and from far-distant Babylon his letters were written. James was the brother of the Lord and the leading figure in the early church at Jerusalem. Jude was probably the brother of James just mentioned and likewise related to the Lord. In their respective letters, James laid emphasis upon works; Peter, upon hope; John, upon love; and Jude, upon judgment.

5. *The Revelation*

The last book of the Bible and the only prophetic book of the New Testament, the Revelation attains and embodies the perfection of apocalyptic literature. It was written by John during his exile on Patmos, a small island in the Aegean Sea, whither he had been banished because of his faith. Addressed primarily to seven of the prominent churches in the Roman province of Asia, the message was designed for the wider circle of Christians in that day and the future. Its meaning, though veiled by symbols, must have been in the main entirely clear to its original readers; and we today through its wondrous pages have a forward look to the consummation of the age, the complete triumph of the good, and the ultimate glory of Jehovah.

TO SUMMARIZE YOUR STUDY

Review chapters 1 and 10. On a map showing the world of the early Christians, color the places Christianity is known to have touched by the time the New Testament writings were completed.

Questions for Review and Examination

CHAPTER 1

1. In what ways did Paul's family background and life in Tarsus help to prepare him for his missionary career?
2. Evaluate the theological training which Paul received under Gamaliel.
3. How could Paul, a Jew, be a Roman citizen? What were some advantages to which his Roman citizenship entitled him?
4. We often think of the Pharisees as despicable, yet there were many good things about Pharisaism. List some assets or advantages which Paul experienced because he was a Pharisee and the son of a Pharisee?

CHAPTER 2

5. Try to put yourself in the place of young Saul, the zealous Pharisee, and give all the reasons which, from that point of view, seem valid reasons for trying to stamp out Christianity.
6. In the experience on the road to Damascus, what did Saul learn about himself? What did he learn about Jesus? What complete about-face resulted from this experience?
7. What part did Ananias have in leading Saul into an understanding and acceptance of his lifework?
8. How did Saul demonstrate his new faith in Damascus and in Jerusalem?

CHAPTER 3

9. Recall Saul's experience in seeking membership in the church in Jerusalem and his later work in the church at Antioch. What part did Barnabas have in leading Saul to find his place in the work of the Lord?
10. Point out what you consider elements of strength in the church at Antioch (in Syria).
11. Name the places where Paul founded churches on his first missionary journey.

CHAPTER 4

12. What, in brief, was the teaching of the Judaizers? How did this teaching differ from the gospel which Paul preached?
13. What was the occasion for the Jerusalem council?
14. By what procedure and through what means did the council at Jerusalem reach its conclusion? What was the place and work of the Holy Spirit in relation to this conclusion?
15. Why was the decision of the Jerusalem council so significant? How was it made known to the various churches?

CHAPTER 5

16. Who was Paul's companion as he began his second missionary journey? Account for the change in the missionary personnel.
17. What four areas of emphasis does the author point out for Paul's second missionary journey?
18. What caused Paul to leave Asia Minor and begin missionary work in Europe? Name two churches founded in Macedonia on Paul's second missionary journey to which he later wrote letters that are now in our Bible.
19. What pattern of events seems to have occurred in each place where Paul did mission work, up to the time he went to Athens?

CHAPTER 6

20. How was the situation in Athens unlike that in the cities which Paul had previously visited as a missionary?
21. What response did Paul get from the Athenians? Do you consider his ministry in Athens a failure?
22. Paul spent eighteen months in Corinth, considered the most corrupt city of Greece. What did the missionary accomplish in this ministry?

CHAPTER 7

23. Paul's ministry of three years' duration at Ephesus was largely a teaching program. What evidences do we find in the Scriptures that this ministry had far-reaching evangelistic results?
24. Tell briefly the story of Christianity's clash with paganism in Ephesus.
25. Letters to what churches were probably written at various places during Paul's third missionary journey?

CHAPTER 8

26. What questions did the Judaizing Christians in Jerusalem raise about Paul's work? What plan was adopted in the hope of improving relationships with these Jewish Christians?

27. What precipitated the riot in the Temple? How was Paul saved from a lynching?

28. Name the various places and the officials before whom Paul was tried after his arrest in Jerusalem and before he was sent to Rome.

CHAPTER 9

29. Name the experiences that Paul and the others aboard ship had on the journey from Caesarea to Rome.

30. Give your opinion of the treatment which the centurian, Julius, accorded Paul on this journey. What firsthand evidence did Julius have to make him believe that Paul was an important person?

31. What were the main ideas Paul tried to get across in his interviews with the Jews in Rome?

32. Name the epistles Paul wrote during his imprisonment in Rome or during the interval between two imprisonments. Which seems to have been his last epistle?

CHAPTER 10

33. Summarize the progress which had been made in carrying out the pattern of Acts 1:8 by the time the last book of the New Testament was written.

	Stoics (Phil)	Epicureans
Theology	Fundamentalist	Liberalists (Sad.)
adherents	Serious-minded	Pleasure-loving
Phil. of Life	Sought truth cold; feeling. ves.	Eat, drink & be merry, pleasure seeking,
Belief	Believed in divine providence	chance ruled
Resurrection	Soul of man re-absorbed in God.	no resurrection
Related to Gospel	Self-righteous, proud (Self-sufficient)	Goal - to have a good time
Evaluation	Best man, made phil. without revelation	Value as a protest against fatalism

Outline of Acts

1. The Church at Jerusalem 1:1-7:60   30-35
2. The Missions Round About 8:1-11:18
3. The Church